30 Minutes or Less

For People Who Don't Have Time To Cook

Compiled By
**Professional Home Economics Teachers
of California, Nevada, Arizona and Utah**

Editor
Gerry Murry Henderson

Graphic Design, Typography and Production
Mike Burk Production Services, Long Beach, CA

Library of Congress Catalog
Card No. 83-072753
ISBN 0-914159-15-1

*30*Minutes or Less

Assembling a cookbook of kitchen tested recipes (by Home Economics Teachers all over California, Arizona, Nevada and Utah), with beautiful photography (contributors below), and getting it "printed to perfection", just takes a lot of work! As the owner of this little company, I remain grateful to the people and companies who contribute many hours of their busy lives to "make this book happen":

◆ Nancy Freeman, our CCC Office Manager, who receives and "computerizes" all recipes, manages all business at CCC, and is still raising a great family!

◆ Gerry Murry Henderson, who teaches full time at Temple City High School, manages a family, and still edits our recipes annually, as only a good Home Economist can do.

◆ Jeremy Bernstein of KNI, Inc., in Anaheim, has printed our books for about ten years now, and has proven himself as an honest, caring businessman.

◆ Doug Herrema, of Huntington Beach, painstakingly thinks through and "plans to perfection" each year our different publications.

◆ Doug Pierce, of Los Angeles, who literally travels all over California, always takes time to "see the larger picture" and gives direction to the books... such as this year's title *30 Minutes Or Less* to fit our busy lives!

◆ Mike Burk, of Long Beach, who patiently listens to all concerned, and then creatively designs the all important front cover and interior pictures.

◆ "Rich" Richardson, Bill Horton, and Bill O'Brien, who each drive long distances to deliver and pick-up books all over California, Arizona, and Nevada, and patiently see each teacher involved in the sales, are the **REAL HEROES** of this little business! (These **ARE** the kind of guys that Tom Brokaw talks about in *The Greatest Generation*!)

◆ Some great American companies and councils contributed the beautiful foods photography: Del Monte Foods of San Francisco, CA; Dole Foods of Westlake Village, CA; Lawry's Foods of Monrovia, CA; the National Cattleman's Beef Association of Chicago, IL; and the National Pork Producers Council of Des Moines, IA.

◆ And a big **THANK YOU** to anyone who purchases one of these books, as part of the proceeds do help support some wonderful teachers, and their programs for students, in your neighborhood. Keep on! You <u>do</u> make a difference!

Sincerely,

Grady W. Reed

Grady W. Reed, Owner, California Cookbook Company

P.S. Please note that although the book is titled *30 Minutes or Less,* **your** "prep time" could vary, as could **your** "cook or bake" time. Also, please note the **RE-ORDER FORM** on page 159.

Table of Contents
Recipes • Contributors • Index

On our Front Cover:
"Well-Dressed Pork" page 104
Courtesy of National Pork Producers Council, Des Moines, IA

Professional Home Economics Teachers

Advisory Committee

Simone Clements
Bret Harte High School, Angels Camp

Carol Delap
Golden West High School, Visalia

Cindy Elledge
Johansen High School, Modesto

Pam Fecchino
Cimarron-Memorial High School
Las Vegas, NV

Pam Ford
Temecula Valley High School, Temecula

Debbie Harvey
Amador Valley High School, Pleasanton

Carol Goddard
Alhambra High School, Alhambra

Donna Hamilton
Del Oro High School, Loomis

Gerry Henderson
Temple City High School, Temple City

Gage Hewes
So. Pasadena High School, So. Pasadena

Grace Hibma
Office of L.A. County Superintendent of
Schools, Consultant Consumer &
Homemaking Education

Donna Hulen, Career Consultant
Los Alamitos High School, Los Alamitos

Dottie Jones
Etiwanda High School, Etiwanda

Mary Lash
Paramount High School, Paramount

Helen Lievre
La Cañada High School, La Cañada

Karen Lopez
San Luis Obispo High School,
San Luis Obispo

Jeri Lundy
Grossmont High School, La Mesa

Darlene Lupul
Tokay High School, Lodi

Dale Matsuno
Bell Gardens High School, Bell Gardens

Doris Oitzman
Victor Valley High School, Victorville

Linda Paskins
Cordova High School, Rancho Cordova

Mary Rector
Valley High School, Las Vegas, NV

Betty Rabin
Sierra Vista Jr. High School, Cyn. Country

April Rosendahl
Chino High School, Chino

Lynda Ruth
La Mirada High School, La Mirada

Marianne Traw
Ball Junior High School, Anaheim

Sonja Tyree
Ayala High School, Chino Hills

Sue Walters
Morse High School, San Diego

Betty Wells
Bidwell Junior High School, Chico

Kathryn P. Whitten
Regional Supervisor
Home Economics Education, Fresno

Appetizers
Salsas • Dips • Beverages

Applesauce Sandwich Snacks
Serves: 4   Prep time: 15 minutes

1 cup applesauce
8 slices bread
$^1/_4$ cup butter or margarine, softened
1 tablespoon sugar
$^1/_4$ teaspoon cinnamon

Spread applesauce on four slices of bread; top with other slice of bread. Lightly butter the outsides of the sandwiches. Toast on a hot griddle for 3 to 4 minutes on each side or until golden brown. Combine sugar and cinnamon; sprinkle over both sides of the sandwiches. Cut into 4 wedges and serve immediately.

"Children love these snacks. Try it with homemade applesauce that you make after a trip to the apple regions of our state."

Dotti Jones   **Etiwanda High School, Rancho Cucamonga, CA**

Bacon Wrapped Artichokes With Dijon Mustard
Serves: 6   Prep time: 5 minutes, Bake: 15 - 20 minutes

8 to 9 slices bacon
1 (16 ounce) can artichokes, in water, quartered
round toothpicks
3 tablespoons Dijon mustard

Preheat oven to 400 degrees. Cover a baking sheet with aluminum foil for easy clean up. Drain artichokes. Cut bacon slices in half. Wrap artichoke with bacon and secure with a toothpick. Place on baking sheet and bake 15 to 20 minutes, or until bacon is crisp. Serve with Dijon mustard, for dipping.

"I got this recipe from The Main Corpse, *by Diane Mott Davidson. My catering classes read this culinary mystery novel as a class requirement."*

Sandra Hughes   **Upland High School, Upland, CA**

BBQ Chicken Quesadilla
Serves: 4   Prep time: 10 minutes, Bake: 10 minutes

1 chicken breast, cooked, cubed
$^1/_2$ cup barbecue sauce
$^1/_4$ cup onion, chopped
$^1/_2$ cup bell pepper, chopped
4 ounces cheddar cheese, grated
8 flour tortillas

Preheat oven to 425 degrees. Place 4 tortillas on cookie sheet. Combine chicken with barbecue sauce and toss to coat. Spread chicken evenly over tortillas. Sprinkle with cheese, peppers and onions. Top with remaining tortillas and bake 8 to 10 minutes. Cool slightly; cut into pizza slices and serve.

"Quick and easy for parties or get-togethers."

Tracie Priske   **Valencia High School, Valencia, CA**

Biscuit Mini Focaccia
Makes: 10   Prep time: 15 minutes, Bake: 10 - 12 minutes

$^1/_2$ cup fresh basil leaves
$^1/_4$ cup fresh thyme sprigs
2 cloves garlic, chopped
$^1/_4$ teaspoon salt (optional)
dash pepper
$^1/_4$ cup olive or vegetable oil
1 (12 ounce) can refrigerator flaky biscuits
$^1/_4$ cup pine nuts
$^1/_3$ cup Parmesan cheese, grated

Preheat oven to 400 degrees. In blender container or food processor with metal blade, combine basil, thyme, garlic, salt, pepper and oil. Cover and blend or process until finely chopped, scraping down sides of container if necessary. Separate biscuit dough into 10 biscuits. On ungreased cookie sheets, press or roll each biscuit to a 3" circle. Make several indentations with fingers in tops of biscuits. Spread about 1 teaspoon basil mixture evenly over each biscuit. Sprinkle with 1 teaspoon pine nuts; press gently. Sprinkle with cheese. Bake 10 to 12 minutes, or until golden brown. Serve warm.

Betty Rabin   **Sierra Vista Junior High School, Canyon Country, CA**

Bruschetta con Pomodori

Serves: 6   Prep time: 5 minutes, Bake: 10 minutes

$^1/_2$ cup olive oil
6 small ripe firm tomatoes, seeded, halved, diced
2 cloves garlic, minced
6 leaves basil, freshly chopped
salt and pepper, to taste
12 ($^1/_2$") slices French bread

Preheat oven to 400 degrees. In a small bowl, combine olive oil, chopped tomatoes and basil. Using a garlic press, add garlic to tomato mixture. Add a pinch of salt and pepper; stir and let rest 30 minutes. Meanwhile, slice bread using serrated knife. Toast or grill bread slices on stoneware or baking sheet in oven, about 10 minutes, or until browned on both sides. Remove from oven and spoon tomato mixture over tops of toasted bread. Serve immediately.

"Great for last minute appetizers. Good with a slice of mozzarella cheese on top.
Use all fresh ingredients in their peak seasons. Quick, easy and delicious."

Patti Bartholomew   **Casa Roble High School, Orangevale, CA**

Canadian Bacon Boboli Pizza

Serves: 4   Prep time: 10 minutes, Bake: 10 - 12 minutes

2 (7") Boboli breads
1 (small) can tomato paste
4 ounces cheddar or mozzarella cheese, shredded
4 slices Canadian bacon, cut up
$^1/_2$ cup pineapple chunks, drained
$^1/_4$ green bell pepper
2 red onions, chopped

Preheat oven to 375 degrees. Place bread on ungreased cookie sheet. Spread tomato paste evenly over bread. Arrange Canadian bacon, pineapple, bell pepper and onion over top. Sprinkle with shredded cheese and bake 10 to 12 minutes, until cheese is melted.

Doris Richmond   **Tulare Western High School, Tulare, CA**

Chafing Dish Meatballs

Serves: 8 - 10   Prep time: 10 minutes, Cook: 30 minutes

Meatballs:
1 pound ground beef
1 small egg, slightly beaten
2 tablespoons onion, grated
salt, to taste
1 slice bread, crumbled
Sauce:
1$^1/_2$ cups chili sauce
1 to 2 tablespoons lemon juice
$^3/_4$ cup grape jelly

Meatballs: Combine ground meat, egg, onion, salt and crumbled bread; mix well. Shape into 1" balls. Cook in large skillet over medium heat just until outside is browned. *Sauce:* Combine chili sauce, lemon juice and grape jelly in medium-sized saucepan. Simmer over medium heat 30 minutes. Add meatballs as soon as they are browned. If desired, transfer meatballs and sauce to a chafing dish.

"The longer the meatballs simmer in the sauce, the better they are."

Laurie Owen   **Challenger Middle School, San Diego, CA**

Cheese & Olive Balls

Serves: 8 - 10   Prep time: 15 minutes, Bake: 15 minutes

2 cups cheddar cheese, grated
1 cup flour
1 teaspoon paprika
1 cube butter, softened
1 (7 ounce) jar green olives

Preheat oven to 400 degrees. Mix grated cheese with flour and paprika. Cut in butter with a pastry blender. From a small ball of dough in your hand. Form a ball of dough around individual olives. Place balls on baking sheet and bake 15 minutes. Serve hot.

"Great party recipe. You can freeze and reheat on the day of the party."

Pat Smith   **Kern Valley High School, Lake Isabella, CA**

Fresh Fruit Smoothie

Serves: 1 - 2   Prep time: 5 minutes

6 ounces yogurt, plain or vanilla
$^3/_4$ cup orange juice
1 banana
1 kiwi or peach, seeded, sliced
1 cup strawberries, frozen

Combine ingredients in a blender and whir until smooth.

"Nutritious, great for kids who won't eat fruit! We have them with popcorn on a 'Mom isn't cooking night'!"

Charlotte Heitzmann   **Mariposa Co. High School, Mariposa, CA**

Hot Artichoke Dip

Makes: 2 ½ cups   Prep time: 10 minutes, Bake: 20 - 25 minutes

     1 cup Miracle Whip
     1 (14 ounce) can artichoke hearts, drained, chopped
     4 ounces Parmesan cheese, grated
     1 clove garlic, minced
     Garnish: chopped tomato, sliced green onions

Preheat oven to 350 degrees. Mix together Miracle Whip, drained artichoke hearts, Parmesan cheese and garlic. Spoon into 9" pie plate and bake 20 to 25 minutes, uncovered, or until lightly browned. Garnish with tomato and green onion. Serve with crackers.

"To make ahead, prepare dip as directed, except for baking. Refrigerate overnight. It's a hit at parties and is simple to make."

Barbara Crampton   **Buena Park High School, Buena Park, CA**

Hot Crab Dip

Makes: 3 cups   Prep time: 10 minutes, Microwave: 5 minutes

     1 (6 ounce) can crab meat
     1 (8 ounce) package cream cheese
     ½ cup Parmesan cheese
     ¼ cup green onion, chopped
     ¼ cup sour cream
     ¼ cup mayonnaise
     1 tablespoon dry parsley flakes
     crackers, chips, or vegetable dippers

Rinse and drain crab meat. Place in 1 quart casserole or microwave safe serving dish. Add remaining ingredients. Cover with lid or waxed paper. Microwave on 70% power 4 to 5 minutes, stirring every 2 minutes, or until dip reaches desired serving temperature.

Rhonda Nelson   **Rancho Santa Margarita IS, Rancho Santa Margarita, CA**

Hot Crab Dip with Salsa

Makes: 3 cups   Prep time: 15 minutes

     8 ounces Neufchatel cheese
     8 ounces nonfat cream cheese
     ½ pound crab meat (imitation or real)
     ½ cup fresh salsa
     2 teaspoons worcestershire sauce

Combine all ingredients in a saucepan and heat thoroughly. Keep warm in oven until ready to serve. Serve with your favorite crackers.

"Fast, easy and great tasting! Low fat too!"

Peg Ellington   **Yucca Valley High School, Yucca Valley, CA**

Luscious Shrimp Spread

Serves: 10 - 12   Prep time: 25 minutes, Chill: 6 - 8 hours

        1 envelope Knox gelatin
        $1/4$ cup hot water
        1 can cream of celery soup
        16 ounces cream cheese
        1 cup mayonnaise
        $3/4$ cup celery, minced
        $3/4$ cup green onion, minced
        2 pounds small shrimp, divided
        Garnish: chopped chives

Spray a jello mold with nonstick cooking spray; set aside. In saucepan, dissolve gelatin in water. Add soup and heat to boiling. Add cream cheese and beat well; cool. Stir in mayonnaise, celery, onion and 1 pound of shrimp. Pour into prepared mold and chill 6 to 8 hours. Remove from mold and garnish with remaining 1 pound shrimp. Sprinkle with chopped chives.

"Fast, easy and great for parties!"

Leilani Neiner   **Fontana High School, Fontana, CA**

Mexican Cheese Puffs

Serves: 6 - 8   Prep time: 20 minutes

        oil, for frying
        6 to 8 flour tortillas
        3 tablespoons green chiles, chopped
        2 tablespoons black olives, chopped
        1 tablespoon onion, chopped
        1 cup jack cheese, grated
        $1/2$ cup salsa
        $1/2$ cup sour cream

Heat 1" oil in a frying pan. Warm tortillas, a few at a time in the microwave to soften. On each tortilla, place $1/2$ teaspoon olives, $1/2$ teaspoon chiles, $1/2$ teaspoon onion, and 2 tablespoons cheese. Fold edges into center, to form a square. Fry in hot oil, seam side down, turning once. Drain on paper towels, serve with salsa and sour cream.

"These are delicious!"

Linda Silvasy   **Olive Peirce Middle School, Ramona, CA**

Mocha Fireside Coffee Mix

Makes: 80 cups   Prep time: 10 minutes

> 2 $1/2$ cups powdered non-dairy creamer
> 2 cups hot cocoa mix
> 1 cup instant coffee
> 1 cup Ovaltine Chocolate Drink Mix
> $1/4$ cup sugar
> 1 tablespoon cinnamon
> 1 teaspoon ground nutmeg

Combine all ingredients in a large plastic ziploc bag; mix well. Store in an airtight container. To make 1 cup, add 4 teaspoons mixture to 1 cup boiling water.

"This tastes so good after a long day at work
It's like what your Mom would make!"

Dotti Jones   **Etiwanda High School, Rancho Cucamonga, CA**

Nachos Now!

Serves: 4   Prep time: 10 minutes

> 3 ounces tortilla chips (about 30 large chips)
> 4 to 6 ounces cheddar or jack cheese, shredded
> $1/2$ teaspoon chili powder
> $1/4$ teaspoon ground cumin
> *Toppings:* sliced olives, jalapeños, sour cream, sliced green onions,
>   chopped bell pepper

Place tortilla chips on microwave safe platter or paper plate. Place shredded cheese in plastic bag with chili powder and cumin. Shake until spices are evenly distributed; sprinkle evenly over chips. Microwave on 50% power 2 minutes, or until cheese melts. Serve plain or with any combination of desired toppings.

"Quick and easy! The spice combination gives a different twist to a classic snack.
For a nacho meal, add cooked shredded beef, pork or chicken."

Laura de la Motte   **Turlock High School, Turlock, CA**

Oyster Cracker Dish

Serves: 5   Prep time: 10 minutes, Bake: 20 minutes

> 1 can oysters, drained
> 20 saltine crackers, crushed
> 1 cube butter or margarine, softened
> pepper, to taste
> 1 can evaporated milk OR heavy cream

Preheat oven to 400 degrees. In a small baking dish, layer one-fourth portion crumbled crackers and oysters, a few tablespoonfuls butter or margarine and dash of pepper. Continue layers until all ingredients are used. Cover with cream and bake 20 minutes, until top is browned. Serve immediately. NOTE: Recipe can be doubled. Adjust crackers or oysters according to individual taste.

"Many thanks to my friend, Julie Santos, for sharing this recipe
She makes it for her son, David, who loves oysters!"

Mary Springhorn   **Anderson High School, Anderson, CA**

Parmesan Rounds
Makes: 25 - 30   **Prep time: 15 minutes**

$^1/_2$ cup mayonnaise
$^1/_2$ cup Parmesan cheese
$^1/_4$ cup green onion, chopped
1 French bread baguette, thinly sliced
Optional: $^1/_2$ cup crab or shrimp, finely chopped

Mix together mayonnaise, Parmesan and green onion. (If using optional seafood, stir into mixture.) Spread mixture on baguette rounds. Broil 2 to 4 minutes, until browned. Serve immediately.

Judy Herman   **Dublin High School, Dublin, CA**

Pineapple Dip
Serves: 8 - 10   **Prep time: 10 minutes, Chill: 1 hour**

2 (8 ounce) packages cream cheese, softened
1 (8.5 ounce) can pineapple, crushed, drained
2 tablespoons green pepper, chopped
2 tablespoons green onion, chopped
$^1/_4$ teaspoon salt

Mix all ingredients together. Form into a ball or balls and refrigerate at least one hour before serving. Serve with crackers.

"A recipe I got from the Prince Edward Island website at Christmas time."

Kathy Warren   **McClatchy High School, Sacramento, CA**

Pizza Joes
Serves: 8   **Prep time: 10 minutes**

8 French sandwich rolls, split
1 (8 ounce) jar pizza sauce
1 (3 ounce) package pepperoni, sliced
8 slices mozzarella cheese
4 to 6 tablespoons Parmesan cheese, grated

Liberally spread each side of the sandwich rolls with pizza sauce. On bottom half of the roll, place 3 to 4 slices pepperoni. Cover with 1 slice mozzarella cheese. Sprinkle with Parmesan cheese. Top with upper half of roll. Wrap in paper napkin and microwave on HIGH 30 to 60 seconds (or wrap in foil and heat 20 to 25 minutes at 350 degrees). Filling should be hot and cheese melted.

Judy Herman   **Dublin High School, Dublin, CA**

Portobello Pizzas

Serves: 4   Prep time: 15 minutes

    4 Portobello mushrooms
    $1/_2$ (14 ounce) jar pizza sauce
    4 ounces mozzarella cheese, grated
    4 ounces salami or pepperoni

Preheat broiler. Scrape inside of mushrooms; clean with mushroom brush. Broil outside of mushrooms about 5 minutes or until softened. Turn over and broil inside, about 2 minutes. Fill with pizza sauce, mozzarella cheese and salami or pepperoni; broil 3 to 4 minutes, or until cheese bubbles.

Gail Hurt-Knieriem   Estancia High School, Costa Mesa, CA

Raw Vegetable Dip

Makes: 2 $2/_3$ cups   Prep time: 10 minutes, Chill: 30 minutes

    1 cup cottage cheese
    1 cup sour cream
    $2/_3$ cup mayonnaise
    1 tablespoon dried minced onion
    1 tablespoon dried parsley
    1 teaspoon dill weed
    1 teaspoon beau monde

Mix all ingredients together. Refrigerate at least 30 minutes to allow flavors to combine.

   "Lowfat and nonfat versions make a healthy dip for raw vegetables."

Cindy Peters   Black Diamond Middle School, Antioch, CA

Salsa With A Twist

Serves: a crowd   Prep time: 15 minutes

    1 (24 ounce) jar Herdez Cosera Salsa, medium
    2 (6 ounce) cans El Patio jalapeño salsa
    2 avocados, peeled, seeded, cubed
    1 bunch green onions, chopped
    1 (small) bunch cilantro, chopped
    1 to 2 cups cheddar and jack cheese combination, grated

Mix together both salsas. Stir in avocado, green onion and cilantro. Gently mix in grated cheese. If you prefer milder salsa, use only 1 can jalapeño salsa.

   *"Once you serve this salsa, you will always be
        asked to bring it to all get-togethers."*

LaRae Harguess   Hesperia High School, Hesperia, CA

Spiced Holiday Nuts

Makes: 1 ¹/₂ cups　　　　　　　　**Prep time: 20 minutes**

　nonstick cooking spray
　2 tablespoons olive oil
　¹/₂ teaspoon ground ginger
　¹/₂ teaspoon curry powder
　¹/₄ teaspoon cayenne pepper
　2 tablespoons sugar
　1 tablespoon honey
　³/₄ cup walnut halves
　³/₄ cup pecan halves
　salt, to taste

Line baking sheet with foil; oil lightly with nonstick cooking spray. Heat olive oil in large nonstick skillet over medium heat. Add ginger, curry powder and cayenne pepper; saute until fragrant, about 5 seconds. Stir in sugar and honey; add nuts and stir until honey mixture is amber in color and nuts are well coated, about 6 minutes. Transfer nut mixture to prepared baking sheet. Working quickly, separate nuts with spoon. Sprinkle with salt. Cool and store in airtight container.

"I also used these chopped and sprinkled over a green salad. Adds a great flavor."

Julie Shelburne　　　　　　　**Tulare Union High School, Tulare, CA**

Stuffed Artichoke Hearts

Serves: 6 - 8　　　**Prep time: 10 minutes, Bake: 5 - 7 minutes**

　1 (large) jar marinated artichoke heart bottoms
　1 (8 ounce) package cream cheese
　Parmesan cheese, freshly grated
　nonstick cooking spray

Preheat oven to 400 degrees. Drain artichoke bottoms and pat dry with paper towel. Place a teaspoon-size dollop of cream cheese in middle of each artichoke bottom. Top with freshly grated Parmesan cheese. Bake on cookie sheet that has been sprayed with nonstick cooking spray 5 to 7 minutes, until cheese is golden brown.

Gail McAuley　　　　　　　**Lincoln High School, Stockton, CA**

Tangy Strawberry Swirl

Serves: 4　　　　　　　　**Prep time: 5 minutes**

　2 cups lowfat buttermilk
　2 cups frozen strawberries
　3 to 4 packages sweetener, or sugar to taste

Blend all ingredients together on high until good and frosty. NOTE: Any frozen fruit may be used in place of strawberries.

"Very refreshing, unique and low in calories and fat."

Susan Heide　　　　**San Gorgonio High School, San Bernardino, CA**
14

Three Pepper Salsa

Makes: 2 cups   Prep time: 30 minutes

  2 large Anaheim chiles
  1 large red bell pepper
  1 cup tomato, diced
  $^1/_2$ cup red onion, diced
  $^1/_4$ cup fresh cilantro, chopped
  3 tablespoons orange juice
  2 tablespoons lime juice
  2 tablespoons serrano chile, seeded, minced
  $^1/_2$ teaspoon crushed red pepper

Preheat broiler. Cut Anaheim chile and bell pepper lengthwise; discard seeds and membranes. (Be careful when handling chiles, use gloves or wash hands thoroughly after handling.) Place skin side up on foil lined baking sheet; flatten with hand. Broil 10 minutes, or until blackened. Place in ziploc bag; seal and let stand 10 minutes. Peel and dice; combine with remaining ingredients. Cover and chill.

"Great for cleaning out the nasal passages!"

Dale Sheehan   **Santana High School, Santee, CA**

Turkey Nachos

Serves: 4   Prep time: 10 minutes

  1 (10.75 ounce) can cheddar cheese soup
  1 cup salsa
  1 (16 ounce) can refried beans
  1 cup turkey or chicken, cooked, diced
  1 (10 or 15 ounce) bag tortilla chips

Mix together condensed soup, salsa and beans in covered casserole. Microwave on HIGH about 6 minutes, stirring after 3 minutes. Stir in cooked turkey or chicken. Microwave, covered about 2 minutes more, until heated through. Serve warm with tortilla chips.

"I just subscribed to 'Taste of Home's Quick Cooking' and adapted one of their recipes for this book. Can be kept on hand for a quick appetizer or snack."

Gail Hurt-Knieriem   **Estancia High School, Costa Mesa, CA**

Soups

Soup • Chili • Chowder

Cheesy Broccoli Soup

Serves: 6   Prep time: 15 minutes

10 ounces broccoli, chopped
$1/_2$ cup water
2 cans cream of potato soup
2 cups milk
2 cups cheddar cheese, shredded

Bring broccoli and water to a boil; cover and simmer 5 minutes. Do not drain water. Stir in potato soup and milk. Stir over medium-high heat 3 to 5 minutes. Add cheese and stir until melted.

"When the weather turns cooler, I keep the basic ingredients for this quick soup in my kitchen."

Doris Oitzman   **Victor Valley High School, Victorville, CA**

Chicken Chile Verde

Serves: 10   Prep time: 10 minutes, Cook: 30 minutes

3 cups chicken, cooked, cubed
1 (28 ounce) can Las Palmas green enchilada sauce
1 (15 to 19 ounce) can black beans, drained, rinsed
1 $1/_4$ cups frozen corn
1 cup onion, chopped
2 cloves garlic, minced
1 tablespoon fresh cilantro, chopped

Combine all ingredients in large saucepan and bring to a boil; simmer 30 minutes.

"So easy and so tasty!"

Carol O'Keefe   **Canyon Hills High School, Anaheim Hills, CA**

16

Chili Chicken Soup

Serves: 4   Prep time: 10 minutes, Cook: 30 - 40 minutes

- 2 cloves garlic, minced
- 1 small can diced green chiles
- 2 (14.5 ounce) cans stewed tomatoes
- 2 (15.5 ounce) cans pinto beans, drained
- $^3/_4$ cup picante sauce
- 1 teaspoon chili powder
- 1 teaspoon cumin
- $^1/_2$ teaspoon salt
- 3 boneless, skinless chicken breast halves, cut into 1" cubes
- 1 cup onion, chopped
- 1 bell pepper, chopped
- *Garnish:* chopped cilantro, chopped black olives, shredded lettuce, shredded cheddar cheese, tortilla chips, sour cream, sliced avocado

In 5 quart soup pot, combine garlic, green chiles, stewed tomatoes, pinto beans, picante sauce and spices and heat over medium heat. Meanwhile, prepare chicken, onion and bell pepper. Add to the pot and heat until chicken is tender, about 30 to 40 minutes. Garnish with desired toppings.

Jill Marsh   **Warren High School, Downey, CA**

Chili Tomato Soup

Serves: 4   Prep time: 5 minutes, Cook: 5 - 10 minutes

- 1 can chili, without beans
- 1 can bean and bacon soup
- 1 can tomato soup
- 1 bag corn chips

Blend chili with soups. Heat in a saucepan, 5 to 10 minutes over medium heat or in a microwave oven 3 to 5 minutes on HIGH, until heated through. Serve over corn chips.

"This recipe was given to me years ago by my good friend,
Pat Jones, a retired Home Economics teacher."

Carol Kagy   **Norwalk High School, Norwalk, CA**

Chili-Meatball and Vegetable Soup

Serves: 6 - 8   Prep time: 20 minutes, Cook: 10 minutes

    1 pound lean ground beef
    $1/4$ cup dry bread crumbs
    $1/4$ cup tomato juice
    4 to 5 teaspoons chili powder
    2 tablespoons minced onion
    $2 1/2$ teaspoons salt, divided
    $1/4$ teaspoon pepper
    2 (10.5 ounce) cans condensed beef broth
    1 (16 ounce) can tomatoes, diced
    1 (10 ounce) package frozen mixed vegetables
    1 medium onion, sliced
    $1/2$ cup instant rice

Preheat oven to 500 degrees. In medium bowl, combine ground beef, bread crumbs, tomato juice, chili powder, minced onion, $1 1/2$ teaspoons salt and pepper. Shape into small balls. Place on lightly greased jellyroll pan and bake 10 minutes. In large kettle, combine beef broth with 2 soup cans of water, tomatoes and their liquid, vegetables, onion, rice and 1 teaspoon salt. Cover and heat to boiling; reduce heat and add meatballs; let simmer 10 minutes.

"This is my son's favorite soup. Do not be afraid to use the full amount of chili powder. It seems to mellow in the soup. I do cut the salt amount, however. Baking meatballs is much easier than frying them."

Eileen Jackson   **Lexington Junior High School, Cypress, CA**

Chinese Chicken Corn Soup

Serves: 6 - 8   Prep time: 30 minutes

    5 cups soup stock
    1 can creamed corn
    1 cup chicken, finely minced
    1 tablespoon white wine
    2 tablespoons cooked ham, finely chopped
    2 tablespoons water chestnuts, finely chopped
    salt and pepper, to taste
    1 tablespoon cornstarch
    $1/4$ cup water
    2 egg whites

Bring stock to boiling; add creamed corn and boil 5 minutes. Stir together minced chicken and wine; add to boiling stock. Mix together ham and water chestnuts; season to taste with salt and pepper and add to boiling stock. Boil about 3 minutes. Mix cornstarch and water together and stir into boiling stock. Beat egg whites until smooth, but not fluffy. Turn off heat under soup. Drizzle egg whites into soup slowly. Mix very slightly and gently. Serve hot. NOTE: May easily be reheated in the microwave or on top of the stove by the cup or bowl.

"I have so many requests for this recipe that I decided to submit it and sell everyone cookbooks! It's a favorite of my 'Hospitality - Food Service' classes."

Peg Ellington   **Yucca Valley High School, Yucca Valley, CA**

Cream of Mushroom Soup

Serves: 4   Prep time: 15 minutes

    10 fresh mushrooms, thinly sliced
    3 tablespoons margarine
    3 tablespoons flour
    1 $1/2$ cups milk
    1 $1/2$ cups water
    2 cubes beef bouillon
    $1/8$ teaspoon nutmeg

In a 1 quart saucepan, saute mushrooms in margarine until they become slightly translucent. Remove from heat. Stir in flour. Gradually stir in milk and water. Add bouillon and nutmeg and heat to a boil, stirring constantly. Serve immediately.

Melissa Webb   **Lakewood High School, Lakewood, CA**

Creamy Zucchini Soup

Serves: 4 - 6   Prep time: 20 minutes

    2 onions, chopped
    3 cloves garlic, minced
    4 tablespoons butter
    8 medium zucchini, sliced
    1 to 2 stalks celery, chopped
    1 large carrot, sliced
    3 cups chicken stock
    2 tablespoons fresh lemon juice

Saute onions and garlic in butter until onions are golden. Add remaining ingredients, except lemon juice. Bring to a boil and simmer 15 to 20 minutes. Cool slightly. Puree soup in blender. Add lemon juice. If necessary, thin with additional chicken stock or white wine. NOTE: Since this is pureed, I just cut ingredients into large pieces to save time.

"A delicious creamy soup without the calories of cream."

Millie Deeton   **Ayala High School, Chino Hills, CA**

Italian Peasant Soup

Serves: 6 - 8   Prep time: 25 minutes

2 (15 ounce) cans chicken broth, low sodium
1 (15 ounce) can crushed tomatoes
1 (15 ounce) can white beans
$1/2$ teaspoon Italian seasoning
1 teaspoon garlic, crushed
1 tablespoon olive oil
$1/2$ cup onion, chopped
1 cup carrots, chopped
2 cups cabbage, chopped
3 cups small ribbon pasta noodles, cooked

In large 4 quart pot, simmer broth, tomatoes, beans, seasoning and garlic. In skillet, heat olive oil over medium-high heat. Saute carrots, onion and cabbage until vegetables are tender. Add sauteed vegetables to soup pot and simmer 5 minutes. Stir in cooked pasta and simmer 10 minutes more.

Kristine Hubbard   **San Luis Obispo High School, San Luis Obispo, CA**

Leek & Potato Soup

Serves: 6 - 8   Prep time: 30 minutes

4 cups potatoes, diced
4 cups leeks, white portion only, sliced
1 quart chicken broth
1 teaspoon salt
1 cup nonfat milk
5 tablespoons powdered nonfat milk
1 tablespoon butter
$1/4$ teaspoon white pepper
Garnish: chopped chives or parsley

Place potatoes and leeks in large saucepan; cover with chicken broth and simmer, covered, until tender. Add salt. Puree mixture in blender or food processor or push through a sieve and return to saucepan. In separate bowl, blend together nonfat and powdered milk; add to soup. Reheat together. Add little butter and white pepper, to taste. Garnish with chopped chives or parsley.

"This quick, hearty soup recipe was given to me by my mom
It's loaded with calcium, nonfat and great with Southern
Biscuit Muffins! A quick and easy homemade meal!"

Sheryl Malone   **Mt. Carmel High School, San Diego, CA**

Pizza Soup

Serves: 4   **Prep time: 10 minutes, Cook: 20 minutes**

1 1/4 cups fresh mushrooms, sliced
1/2 cup onion, finely chopped
1 teaspoon vegetable oil
2 cups water
1 (15 ounce) can pizza sauce
1 cup pepperoni, chopped
1 cup fresh tomatoes, chopped
1/2 cup Italian sausage, cooked
1/4 teaspoon Italian seasoning
1/4 cup Parmesan cheese, grated
Garnish: Mozzarella cheese, shredded

Cook sausage in small skillet; drain off oil, set sausage aside. In a large saucepan, saute mushrooms and onion in oil for 2 to 3 minutes or until tender. Add water, pizza sauce, pepperoni and Italian seasoning. Bring to a boil over medium heat. Reduce heat; cover and simmer 20 minutes, stirring occasionally. Before serving, stir in Parmesan cheese. Garnish with mozzarella cheese.

Kathie Baczynski   **Mt. Carmel High School, Poway, CA**

Potato Soup

Serves: 6   **Prep time: 30 minutes**

4 large potatoes, peeled, cubed
2 cups water
1 teaspoon dried minced onion
1 clove garlic, minced
1/2 teaspoon salt
1/4 teaspoon pepper
1 cup milk
4 ounces processed American cheese, cubed
2 tablespoons butter
1 tablespoon chicken bouillon granules
1 teaspoon fresh parsley, minced

In large saucepan, combine potatoes, water, onion, garlic salt and pepper; bring to a boil over medium heat. Reduce heat; cover and simmer 15 to 20 minutes or until potatoes are tender. Do not drain. Mash potatoes in liquid until almost smooth. Add remaining ingredients; cook and stir until cheese is melted.

"I add 1/3 cup chopped ham or cooked bacon bits to add a different flavor."

Jeanette Atkinson   **Brinley Middle School, Las Vegas, NV**

Quick Chicken Soup

Makes: 6 $\frac{1}{2}$ cups   Prep time: 30 - 35 minutes

  2 boneless, skinless chicken breast halves
  1 tablespoon oil
  $\frac{1}{4}$ cup shallots, finely chopped
  1 (49.5 ounce) can chicken broth
  $\frac{1}{2}$ cup celery, finely diced
  $\frac{1}{2}$ cup frozen peas
  $\frac{1}{2}$ cup carrots, finely chopped
  1 teaspoon salt
  $\frac{1}{8}$ teaspoon marjoram
  $\frac{1}{8}$ teaspoon thyme
  black pepper, to taste
  3 ounces egg noodles, uncooked

Brown chicken breast meat in large preheated saucepan, with oil, for about 5 minutes. Remove chicken and reduce heat to low. Add shallots and saute 1 to 2 minutes; do not brown. Return chicken to pan and add remaining ingredients, except noodles; bring to a boil. Reduce heat to low, simmer and cook, uncovered 20 minutes or until chicken is tender. Remove chicken, dice and return to pan. Bring soup to a boil; add noodles and cook until noodles are tender.

"Great with a packaged salad and French bread for a quick, good meal."

Liz Aschenbrenner   **Sierra High School, Manteca, CA**

Quick Deli Turkey Soup

Serves: 4   Prep time: 30 minutes

  1 (13.75 ounce) can chicken broth, ready-to-serve
  1 (14.5 ounce) can stewed tomatoes
  1 small zucchini, chopped (about 1 cup)
  $\frac{1}{4}$ teaspoon dried basil leaves, crushed
  $\frac{1}{2}$ pound Butterball Deli turkey breast, cubed
  $\frac{1}{2}$ cup pasta or macaroni, cooked

Combine broth, tomatoes with juice, zucchini and basil in large saucepan. Bring to a boil over high heat. Reduce heat to low; simmer 10 minutes or until zucchini is tender. Stir in turkey and pasta. Continue heating until turkey is heated through.

"From Favorite Name Cookbook*"*

Angela Cruz-Trujillo   **Valley View High School, Moreno Valley, CA**

Quick & Hearty Ramen Soup

Serves: 4   Prep time: 10 minutes, Cook: 20 minutes

 6 cups water
 2 to 3 carrots, peeled, sliced
 2 stalks celery, sliced
 2 packages ramen noodle soup, (any flavor) with seasoning packets
 $1/4$ to $1/2$ teaspoon sesame oil (optional)
 few drops chili oil (optional)
 2 to 3 cups leftover meat
 additional fresh, frozen or canned vegetables (optional)

In a 2 quart pot, bring water to a boil. Add sliced vegetables and let water return to a boil. Break noodles in half and add to pot. Simmer until noodles reach desired doneness. Add seasoning packets and oils, along with meat. Allow soup to heat through. Serve with bread and a salad for a quick, easy meal.

"This is a family favorite using leftover barbecued meats such as steak, pork, or chicken. We have even made it on camping trips."

Laura de la Motte   **Turlock High School, Turlock, CA**

Spicy Southwest Chowder

Serves: 4 - 6   Prep time: 10 minutes, Cook: 15 minutes

 1 (14.5 ounce) can chopped tomatoes
 8 ounces corn, frozen
 1 (10.5 ounce) can chicken broth
 1 (15 ounce) can black beans, drained and rinsed
 1 (4.5 ounce) can diced green chiles
 1 (6 ounce) bag popcorn shrimp, frozen
 $1/2$ cup salsa
 $1/4$ cup tequila
 1 teaspoon cumin
 $1/2$ teaspoon garlic powder
 $1/4$ teaspoon white pepper
 Garnish: chopped cilantro, grated cheese

Mix all ingredients together in a 3 quart saucepan; bring to a boil. Reduce heat and simmer 15 minutes. Serve with garnish, as desired.

"This simple soup can easily be changed to fit your taste. Option for chicken in place of shrimp. Use V-8 juice in lieu of chicken broth, etc."

Joye Cantrell   **Rialto High School, Rialto, CA**

Taco Soup

Serves: 6   Prep time: 10 minutes, Cook: 15 - 20 minutes

- 1 pound hamburger
- 1 medium onion, chopped
- 1 can red kidney beans, undrained
- 1 can string beans, undrained
- 1 large can crushed tomatoes
- 1 can corn, undrained
- 1 can tomato sauce
- 1 package taco seasoning
- *Garnish:* tortilla or Fritos corn chips, grated cheese

Brown hamburger and onion together in large skillet; drain excess fat. Add remaining ingredients and simmer 15 to 20 minutes. Serve over tortilla chips or Fritos corn chips. Sprinkle with grated cheese.

"This recipe is quick and great on a cool day."

Anita Cornwall   **Cimarron-Memorial High School, Las Vegas, NV**

Wild Rice Soup

Serves: 6   Prep time: 15 minutes

- 6 tablespoons butter
- 1 tablespoon minced onion
- $1/2$ cup flour
- 3 cups chicken broth
- 2 cups wild rice, cooked
- $1/3$ cup ham, minced
- $1/2$ cup carrots, finely grated
- 3 tablespoons almonds, slivered
- $1/2$ teaspoon salt
- 1 cup half & half
- 2 tablespoons sherry (optional)
- *Garnish:* minced parsley or chives

Melt butter in a 4 or 6 quart saucepan; add onion and saute until tender. Blend in flour, cooking until bubbly. Add broth, cooking mixture until it comes to a boil. Boil 1 minute. Stir in rice, ham, carrots, almonds and salt. Simmer 5 minutes. Blend in half & half and sherry. Heat to serving temperature. Garnish with parsley or chives.

"I received this recipe from a friend after a day of skiing.
Serve it with warm rolls. Delicious!"

Carla Escola   **Ripon High School, Ripon, CA**

Yam & Apple Soup

Serves: 4   Prep time: 30 minutes

- 1 1/4 teaspoons cumin
- 1 cup chicken broth
- 1 cup water
- 2 tablespoons frozen apple juice concentrate
- 1 pound yams, peeled, cut into chunks
- 1 large Granny Smith apple, peeled, cut into chunks
- 1 (medium) onion, cut into chunks
- 1/4 teaspoon ground pepper
- 1/8 teaspoon cinnamon
- 1/2 cup nonfat milk
- 2 tablespoons plain nonfat yogurt
- 1 tablespoon Italian parsley, chopped

In a Dutch oven or flameproof casserole, cook cumin over medium heat, shaking and stirring pan frequently, until it is fragrant and toasted, 4 to 5 minutes. Add chicken broth, water, apple juice concentrate, yams, apple, onion, pepper and cinnamon; cover and bring to a boil over high heat. Reduce heat to medium-low and simmer until yams and apple are tender, about 20 minutes. Transfer soup to a food processor or blender and puree. Return puree to pan and add milk. Cook, stirring over medium heat, until heated through. Ladle soup into bowls; top with yogurt and sprinkle with chopped parsley.

"A gourmet quality recipe!"

Faith Gobuty   **Woodside High School, Woodside, CA**

Salads

Salad • Dressing • Slaw

Apple Nut Tossed Salad

Serves: 4   Prep time: 15 minutes

3 tablespoons olive oil
1 teaspoon Dijon mustard
$^3/_4$ teaspoon sugar
salt and pepper, to taste
$^1/_2$ cup apple, chopped
1 tablespoon green onion, chopped
3 cups Bibb lettuce, torn
1 to 2 tablespoons walnuts, chopped
1 to 2 tablespoons bleu cheese, crumbled

In a salad bowl, whisk together oil, mustard, sugar, salt and pepper.
Add apple and onion; toss to coat. Add lettuce, walnuts and bleu
cheese; toss gently and serve.

"Very different and refreshing!"

Rebecca Harshbarger   **Temecula Valley High School, Temecula, CA**

Belmont Shore Italian Dressing

Makes: 2 cups   Prep time: 5 - 10 minutes, Chill: 8 hours

1 cup Campbell's beef consomme
16 ounces Best Foods mayonnaise
4 cloves garlic, minced
2 tablespoons red wine vinegar
2 teaspoons coarse black pepper

Mix ingredients together and let set 8 hours. You must use the name
brand products to achieve desired taste. Also, use only 1 cup
consomme - you will have some leftover in can - use it for something
else! Serving suggestion: Serve over a salad consisting of black olives,
tomatoes and romaine lettuce.

"This has been one of my favorite recipes since the 60's.
(Nothing like aging myself!)"

Brenda Burke   **Mt. Whitney High School, Visalia, CA**

Black Bean Salsa Salad

Serves: 4 - 6   Prep time: 30 minutes

    2 cans black beans, drained
    2 cups kernel corn
    1 yellow bell pepper, chopped
    1 red bell pepper, chopped
    1 medium red onion, chopped
    2 large Roma tomatoes, seeded, chopped
    $3/4$ cup fresh cilantro, chopped
    $1/3$ cup fresh parsley, chopped
    2 fresh jalapeño peppers, seeded, chopped
    2 cloves garlic, minced
    2 to 3 tablespoons lime juice, to taste
    1 to 2 tablespoons ground cumin, to taste
    1 tablespoon sugar
    1 teaspoon salt
    pepper, to taste
    1 teaspoon dried oregano
    Garnish: shredded lettuce, tortilla chips, lime wedges

Toss the first 8 ingredients together in large bowl. Stir remaining
ingredients together and pour over bean mixture to coat. Serve over
shredded lettuce with tortillas. Garnish with lime wedges.

"A very colorful summer salad."

Sandy Massey   **Mountain View High School, El Monte, CA**

Broccoli Salad

Serves: 6 - 8   Prep time: 15 minutes

    1 $1/2$ pounds broccoli, finely chopped
    1 small red onion, chopped
    1 cup raisins
    10 strips bacon, cooked and crumbled
    1 cup mayonnaise
    $1/4$ cup sugar
    1 tablespoon vinegar
    1 cup sunflower seeds, shelled

In large bowl, combine broccoli, onion, raisins, and bacon. In small
bowl, combine mayonnaise, sugar and vinegar. Just before serving,
toss dressing with salad. Sprinkle with sunflower seeds.

"This is a popular potluck salad. Everyone loves it and always wants the recipe!"

Libby Newman   **West Valley High School, Hemet, CA**

Broccoli Slaw
Serves: 6   Prep time: 15 minutes

    1 pound bag broccoli cole slaw
    4 green onions, chopped
    1 cup golden raisins
    1 cup Miracle Whip or mayonnaise
    $1/2$ cup sugar
    1 tablespoon vinegar
    1 cup whole cashews

In large bowl, combine broccoli slaw, green onions and raisins. Mix together Miracle Whip or mayonnaise, sugar and vinegar, and add to broccoli cole slaw. Just before serving add cashews.

Susan Lefler   **Ramona Junior High School, Chino, CA**

Chicken Broccoli Pasta Salad
Serves: 6   Prep time: 30 minutes

    8 ounces pasta
    4 tablespoons oil, divided
    2 boneless, skinless chicken breast halves, cut into 1" cubes
    1 stalk broccoli, chopped
    1 onion, chopped
    $1/2$ green pepper, chopped
    Salt 'n Spice, to taste

Cook pasta according to package directions; rinse with cold water and set aside. In wok or large skillet, heat 2 tablespoons oil over high heat. Stir-fry chicken until no longer pink; remove and set aside. Add 2 tablespoons oil to wok and stir-fry broccoli, onion and green pepper until tender crisp. In large bowl, combine cooked pasta with chicken and vegetables. Season with Salt 'n Spice, to taste. Serve warm.

"A student in foods class, Nancy Xiong, shared this in class, they loved it!"

Mary Mondientz   **Buchanan High School, Clovis, CA**

Chicken Salad Canton
Serves: 2 - 4   Prep time: 15 minutes

    1 cup fresh Chinese snow peas or 1 (6 ounce) package
        frozen snow peas, thawed
    1 (14.5 ounce) can Del Monte Diced Tomatoes with Garlic & Onion
    3 tablespoons oil
    3 tablespoons cider vinegar
    1 tablespoon low salt soy sauce
    4 cups cabbage or iceberg lettuce, shredded
    1 cup chicken, cooked, cubed
    pepper, to taste
    Garnish: $1/3$ cup cilantro, chopped or $1/3$ cup sliced green onion,
        toasted sesame seeds

28

Dip fresh snow peas in boiling water $1/2$ minute (do not dip frozen snow peas); cool. Drain tomatoes, reserving $1/4$ cup liquid. Combine reserved liquid with oil, vinegar and soy sauce. Toss dressing and tomatoes with remaining ingredients. Season with pepper, if desired. Garnish with chopped cilantro, sliced green onions and toasted sesame seeds, if desired.

Del Monte Foods San Francisco, CA

Chinese Chicken Noodle Salad
Serves: 4 Prep time: 20 minutes

1 (8 ounce) package salad mix, with cabbage, carrots, red cabbage
2 packages Top Ramen noodles (reserve 1 packet for dressing;
    save other packet for another use)
2 boneless, skinless chicken breast halves, cooked, sliced
Dressing:
2 tablespoons soy sauce
$1/4$ cup rice vinegar
$1/4$ teaspoon ginger
1 seasoning packet from Top Ramen noodles
$1/2$ teaspoon garlic
Garnish: 1 $1/2$ ounces sesame seeds, toasted

In large bowl, break up Top Ramen noodles; add salad mix and cooked chicken; set aside. In a jar with tight fitting lid, shake together dressing ingredients. Pour dressing over salad and toss. Top with toasted sesame seeds and serve.

"Great for leftover chicken or turkey."

Becky Oppen Dana Hills High School, Dana Point, CA

Cranberry Salad
Serves: 8 Prep time: 15 minutes

$1/3$ cup cranberry juice cocktail
$1/3$ cup seasoned rice wine vinegar
$1/3$ cup oil
1 tablespoon honey
1 teaspoon Dijon mustard
1 shallot, minced
$1/4$ cup dried cranberries
10 cups fancy salad greens, rinsed
$1/3$ cup red onion, thinly sliced
salt, to taste
$1/4$ cup cilantro, chopped
2 cups cabbage or radicchio, shredded

In a food processor or blender, puree juice, vinegar, oil, honey, mustard and shallots. Add dried cranberries to dressing (do not blend). In a large shallow bowl, mix salad greens with red onion and dressing. Add salt, to taste. Toss in cilantro and shredded cabbage or radicchio, if desired.

"Red cranberries are an unexpected treat. Especially fun during the holidays."

Liz Coleman   **Oroville High School, Oroville, CA**

Curried Chicken Pineapple Rice Salad
Serves: 6   Prep time: 30 minutes

3 cups Dole Fresh Pineapple Chunks
3 cups brown or white rice, cooked
2 cups chicken, cooked, cubed
$3/4$ cup Dole Celery, sliced
$1/3$ cup green onions, sliced
$1/2$ teaspoon salt
$1/8$ teaspoon pepper
$1/4$ cup chicken broth
2 teaspoons curry powder
$1/4$ cup fat free or reduced calorie honey mustard salad dressing
2 teaspoons lemon juice

Combine pineapple, rice, chicken, celery, green onion, salt and pepper in large bowl. In a microwave safe bowl, combine chicken broth with curry powder. Microwave on HIGH 45 seconds or until hot. Cool slightly. Stir in salad dressing and lemon juice. Pour curry dressing over salad; toss to evenly coat.

Dole Foods   **Westlake Village, CA**

Easy Gourmet Lemon Salad
Serves: 4 - 6   Prep time: 10 minutes

1 head romaine lettuce, cleaned, chopped
3 tablespoons olive oil
juice of 1 to 2 lemons
garlic powder, to taste
$1/3$ cup bleu cheese, crumbled

Coat sides of wooden salad bowl with olive oil. Shake desired amount of garlic powder into oil. Put in lettuce and blue cheese. Squeeze juice of 1 lemon over top and toss to completely coat. Squeeze more lemon, if desired. Serve immediately, to avoid wilting.

"This salad adds a lot of flare to an ordinary meal
Serve with crusty bread as a light lunch or with an entree for your main meal."

Delaine Smith   **West Valley High School, Cottonwood, CA**

Eloise's Fruit Salad Dressing

Serves: 6   Prep time: 10 minutes

    6 ounces limeade frozen concentrate
    $^1/_3$ cup honey
    $^1/_3$ cup oil
    poppy seeds
    6 to 8 cups fresh fruit, diced (oranges, apples, celery, pecans, bananas, etc.)

Place all ingredients in container with lid. Shake or pour over fruit salad, toss. The limeade will keep the apples and bananas from turning brown.

"This is a family favorite from my mother-in-law from Oklahoma, Served at Christmas time with ham."

Sonja Tyree   **Ayala High School, Chino Hills, CA**

Frog Eyed Salad

Serves: 6 - 8   Prep time: 30 minutes, Chill: 1 hour

    $^1/_2$ package Acini de Pepe, uncooked
    1 egg
    $^1/_2$ cup sugar
    1 tablespoon flour
    $^1/_4$ teaspoon salt
    1 (15.25 ounce) can crushed pineapple, drained (reserve juice)
    1 (16 ounce) can fruit cocktail, drained
    1 cup miniature marshmallows
    1 cup whipping cream, whipped

Prepare Acini de Pepe as package directs. In heavy saucepan, beat egg with wire whisk until foamy. Stir in sugar, flour, salt and reserved pineapple juice. Cook over low heat until thickened. In a large bowl, combine the Acini de Pepe with egg mixture. Chill 1 hour. Stir in pineapple, fruit cocktail and marshmallows; fold in whipped cream. Cover and chill thoroughly before serving.

"A friend's recipe. Try it and you will be amazed at how delicious it is."

Sharron Maurice   **Blythe Middle School, Blythe, CA**

Green and Apple Salad

Serves: 4   Prep time: 30 minutes

    1 medium red apple
    2 tablespoons lemon juice
    $1/2$ cup water
    Dressing:
    1 tablespoon + 1 teaspoon salad oil
    $1 \, 1/2$ tablespoons lemon juice
    1 tablespoon fresh mint, chopped
    1 teaspoon honey
    $1/2$ teaspoon garlic salt
    $1/8$ teaspoon pepper
    Salad:
    2 ounces alfalfa sprouts
    $1 \, 1/2$ cups lettuce (iceberg and green leaf)
    $1/8$ cup parsley, finely chopped
    $1/8$ cup green onion, sliced
    $1/2$ cup celery, sliced
    Garnish: $1/4$ cup chopped nuts

Core, but do not peel apple. Cut apple into $1/2$" cubes and immerse in small bowl with mixture of 2 tablespoons lemon juice and $1/2$ cup water; set aside. In a small bowl, beat together the salad oil, lemon juice, mint leaves, honey, garlic salt and pepper until well blended; chill at least 25 minutes to allow flavors to blend. In a 3 quart salad bowl, combine alfalfa spouts, lettuce, parsley, onions and celery. Drain apple and combine with salad. Stir salad dressing well and pour over salad. Toss until all ingredients are well coated. Garnish with chopped nuts and serve.

"Once it's tossed, the colorful salad won't wilt as quickly as most. The varied textures and great flavors make this a favorite salad."

Judy Henry   **Newhart Middle School, Mission Viejo, CA**

Holiday Salad

Serves: 4 - 6   Prep time: 10 minutes

    1 (16 ounce) can whole cranberry sauce, chilled
    1 (8 ounce) package trail mix, without bananas, chilled
    $1/4$ cup pecans or walnuts, chopped (optional)
    1 (12 ounce) carton light whipped topping, thawed
    4 slices fresh lemon, thinly sliced

Thoroughly chill cranberry sauce and trail mix. In a bowl, break up cranberry sauce and mix together with trail mix. Carefully fold in whipped topping. Garnish bowl with lemon slices (4 slices are plenty as you want just a hint of flavor). NOTE: Best if eaten the same day.

"Super easy - elegant for your holiday table and delicious!"

Alice OKeeffe   **Walnut High School, Walnut, CA**

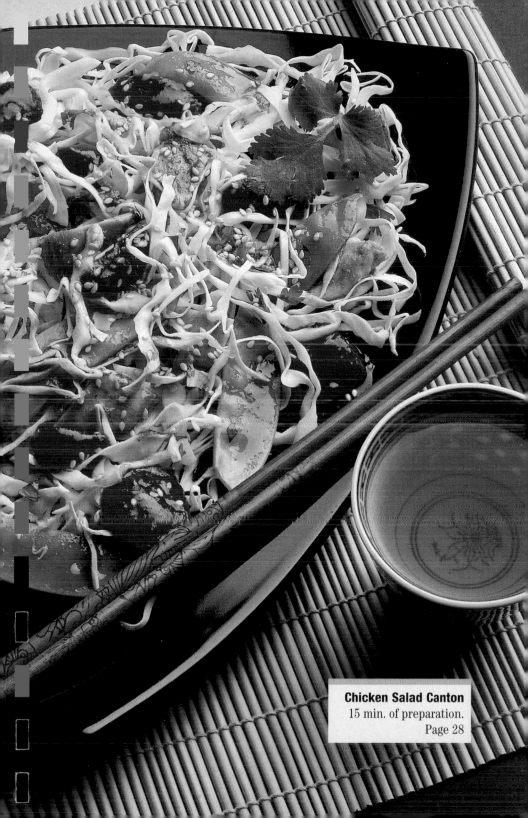

Chicken Salad Canton
15 min. of preparation.
Page 28

Curried Chicken Pineapple Rice Salad
30 min. of preparation.
Page 30

Last Minute Salad

Serves: 8 - 10   Prep time: 10 minutes, Chill: 20 minutes

- 1 envelope whipped topping, prepared
- 1 can apricot pie filling
- 1 to 2 bananas, peeled, sliced
- 1 can red or white cherries, drained
- 1 (small) can pineapple chunks, drained
- 1 can Mandarin oranges, drained
- *Garnish:* maraschino cherries, fresh mint sprigs

Prepare whipped topping as directed on package. Gently fold all ingredients together. Pour into a pretty salad bowl and chill about 20 minutes. Garnish with maraschino cherries and fresh mint, if desired.

"This quick salad can also be served as a dessert."

Lindy Cooper   **Simi Valley High School, Simi Valley, CA**

Layered Green Salad

Serves: 8 - 10   Prep time: 15 minutes, Chill: overnight

- 1 head lettuce, shredded
- $1/_2$ cup green onion, chopped
- 2 cans water chestnuts, sliced
- 1 cup celery, sliced
- 1 package frozen green peas
- 2 cups mayonnaise
- $1/_2$ teaspoon garlic salt
- $1 1/_2$ teaspoons seasoned salt
- *Garnish:* bacon bits, tomato wedges

Layer ingredients in large glass bowl in order listed above (except garnish). Cover and refrigerate overnight. When ready to serve, toss thoroughly and garnish with bacon bits and tomato wedges.

"This is a great dish for potluck functions or for large family gatherings."

Margaret McLeod   **Nogales High School, La Puente, CA**

My Grandmother's Salad

Serves: 4   Prep time: 10 minutes

- 1 cup mandarin oranges, drained
- 1 cup miniature marshmallows
- 1 cup pineapple tidbits, drained
- 1 cup coconut, shredded
- 1 cup sour cream

Mix all ingredients together and serve. NOTE: If ingredients are chilled, can be served right away!

"I got this recipe from my grandmother 30 years ago! Better if chilled overnight."

Gayle Grigg   **Hendrix Junior High School, Chandler, AZ**

Oh So Good Chicken Salad

Serves: 6 - 8   Prep time: 15 minutes

3 boneless, skinless chicken breasts, cooked, cut into bite-sized pieces
1 head iceberg lettuce, cut into bite-sized pieces
4 scallions, chopped
4 ribs celery, chopped
$1/2$ cup cilantro, finely chopped
1 (large) can chow mein noodles
$1/2$ cup peanuts
2 tablespoons hoisin sauce
2 tablespoons sesame oil
$1/2$ cup red wine vinegar
$1/3$ cup honey
$1/2$ cup salad oil
$1/4$ teaspoon salt

In large bowl, combine chicken with lettuce. Add scallions, celery, cilantro, noodles and peanuts; toss well. In blender, mix together hoisin sauce, sesame oil, vinegar, honey, salad oil and salt. Pour dressing over salad and toss just before serving.

"All of our Home Economics students at Mt. Whitney select a CRE for their mid-term project. This was one of the outstanding recipes demonstrated."

Brenda Burke   **Mt. Whitney High School, Visalia, CA**

Oriental Cabbage Salad

Serves: 8   Prep time: 20 minutes

2 tablespoons sesame seeds
$1/2$ cup almonds, sliced
1 tablespoon butter
$3/4$ head cabbage, shredded
1 bunch green onions, sliced
1 package chicken Top Ramen noodles, crushed
Dressing:
1 flavor packet from Top Ramen noodles
2 tablespoons sugar
$1/2$ cup vegetable oil, or less
3 tablespoons rice vinegar
1 tablespoon sesame oil
$1/4$ teaspoon pepper

Saute sesame seeds and almonds in butter until golden brown; set aside. Mix together cabbage, green onions and toasted seeds with crushed noodles. Combine dressing ingredients and toss with salad just before serving.

"I take this salad whenever I am asked to bring one. Always a hit."

Adriana Molinaro   **Granite Hills High School, El Cajon, CA**

34

Orange Cool Whip Salad
Serves: 8   Prep time: 5 minutes

    1 (small) package orange jello
    1 pint cottage cheese
    1 (11 ounce) can mandarin oranges
    1 (20 ounce) can pineapple tidbits
    1 large container Cool Whip

Sprinkle jello over cottage cheese in a bowl and stir until well mixed. Drain oranges and pineapple tidbits; add to cottage cheese mixture. Stir in Cool Whip. Best if refrigerated overnight.

Pat Smith   **Kern Valley High School, Lake Isabella, CA**

Pistachio Fruit Salad
Serves: 8 - 10   Prep time: 15 minutes

    1 (20 ounce) can crushed pineapple, in pineapple juice
    1 (small) package pistachio pudding
    1 (11 ounce) can mandarin oranges, well drained
    1 (12 ounce) container Cool Whip

Place pineapple with juice into a large bowl; sprinkle with dry pudding mix. Let stand 5 minutes, or until mixture thickens. Stir in mandarin oranges and fold in Cool Whip. Refrigerate.

"Calories for this recipe can be reduced if nonfat or low fat Cool Whip is used in place of the regular Cool Whip."

Laurie Owen   **Challenger Middle School, San Diego, CA**

Rancho Taco Chicken Salad
Serves: 8   Prep time: 25 minutes

    1 tablespoon oil
    1 pound boneless, skinless chicken breast halves
    $1/2$ package taco seasoning
    1 package salad greens OR 1 head lettuce, chopped
    1 cup salsa
    1 cup ranch dressing
    1 to 1 $1/2$ cups cheddar cheese, shredded
    Garnish: crushed tortilla chips

Heat oil in skillet over medium heat. Cut chicken into bite-sized pieces and season with taco seasoning. Saute in oil about 8 minutes, or until cooked through. In large bowl, toss greens with chicken, salsa, ranch dressing, and cheese. Sprinkle with crushed chips before serving.

"This recipe can easily be made low fat by using fat free dressing and cheese."

Anita Cornwall   **Cimarron-Memorial High School, Las Vegas, NV**

Southwest Caesar Salad

Serves: 4   Prep time: 10 minutes

  1 (10 ounce) package DOLE Fat Free Complete Caesar Salad
  2 cups chicken breast, cooked, cubed
  1 (14 to 16 ounce) can low-sodium kidney, black or pinto beans, drained
  1 (8 ounce) can low-sodium whole kernel corn, drained
  1 medium tomato, cut into wedges
  1 medium DOLE red, yellow or green bell pepper, thinly sliced
  $1/2$ medium onion, thinly sliced

Combine romaine, croutons and Parmesan cheese from salad bag
with chicken, beans, corn, tomato, bell pepper and onion in large
serving bowl. Pour dressing from packet over salad; toss to evenly
coat.

Dole Foods   **Westlake Village, CA**

Spinach Salad

Serves: 4   Prep time: 20 minutes

  6 slices bacon
  1 $1/2$ pounds fresh spinach
  3 eggs, hard cooked, peeled, chopped
  2 $1/2$ tablespoons onion, chopped
  1 teaspoon salt
  $1/2$ teaspoon pepper
  2 tablespoons olive oil
  1 to 2 tablespoons wine vinegar
  1 tablespoon chicken stock
  pinch curry powder

Fry bacon until crisp; drain, reserving drippings. Wash spinach, drain
and remove stems. Place in large bowl. Crumble bacon over spinach.
Top with chopped eggs and onion. Season with salt and pepper. Heat
bacon drippings with oil, vinegar, chicken broth and curry powder
until hot. Pour over salad and toss. NOTE: You can add cooked
chicken to this salad to make it a main dish.

"Great salad and very impressive."

Beverly Ranger   **Carpinteria High School, Carpinteria, CA**

Strawberry Spinach Salad

Serves: 6 - 8   Prep time: 15 minutes

  $1/3$ cup reduced calorie mayonnaise
  $1/4$ cup orange juice
  1 teaspoon sugar
  1 teaspoon poppy seeds
  $1/2$ pound fresh spinach, washed, trimmed, torn
  2 cups fresh strawberries, sliced

Combine mayonnaise, orange juice, sugar and poppy seeds in a bowl.

Stir well and set aside. Gently toss spinach with strawberries in a large bowl; arrange 8 individual salad plates. Drizzle poppy seed dressing over each salad.

"Best when strawberries are in season, of course!"

Carrie Vaughn   **Cypress High School, Cypress, CA**

Taco Salad

Serves: 6 - 8   Prep time: 20 minutes

    1 1/2 pounds ground beef
    1 package taco seasoning mix
    1 (small) can tomato sauce
    1 (small) can creamed corn
    1 (small) package Fritos corn chips
    1 head lettuce, shredded
    1/2 pound sharp cheddar cheese, grated
    1 (medium) onion, diced
    2 tomatoes, diced
    1 (small) can olives, sliced

Brown ground beef in skillet; drain well. Add taco seasoning mix, tomato sauce and creamed corn. Cook together 5 minutes, stirring occasionally. In large salad bowl, layer corn chips, lettuce, tomatoes, onion and meat. Sprinkle cheese over top and garnish with tomatoes and olives.

"Quick, easy potluck dish. Always a hit with the teenage crowd!"

Judy Dobkins   **Redlands High School, Redlands, CA**

Tarragon Salad

Serves: 4 - 6   Prep time: 15 minutes

    1 large head Romaine lettuce, washed, cut up
    4 green onions, sliced
    6 mushrooms, sliced
    1/2 to 3/4 cup slivered almonds, toasted
    1 (small) can mandarin oranges, drained
    Dressing:
    1/3 cup rice vinegar
    1/2 cup oil
    1 teaspoon salt
    3 tablespoons sugar
    1 teaspoon tarragon

In large salad bowl, combine lettuce, green onion, mushrooms, almonds and oranges. Using a jar with tight fitting lid, combine dressing ingredients and shake well. Toss dressing with salad and serve at once.

Charlotte Runyan   **Saddleback High School, Santa Ana, CA**

Tomato French Dressing

Makes: 2 $1/4$ cups   Prep time: 5 minutes

    1 (10.75 ounce) can tomato soup
    $1/4$ cup vinegar
    $1/2$ cup salad oil
    1 tablespoon + 1 teaspoon onion, minced
    2 tablespoons sugar
    2 teaspoons dry mustard
    1 teaspoon salt
    $1/4$ teaspoon pepper
    1 clove garlic, crushed

Combine all ingredients in a 1 quart jar with tight-fitting lid. Shake well before using.

"This keeps forever in the refrigerator if it gets lost in the back."

Lucille Bell   **Quartz Hill High School, Quartz Hill, CA**

Tropical Salad with Salmon

Serves: 4   Prep time: 25 minutes

    1 avocado, peeled, diced
    1 tablespoon fresh lemon juice
    2 cups cucumber, peeled, diced
    2 cups cantaloupe, peeled, diced
    2 tablespoons fresh chives, snipped
    2 tablespoons fresh dill, chopped
    1 tablespoon shallots, chopped
    3 tablespoons olive oil, divided
    3 tablespoons orange juice, divided
    2 teaspoons honey, divided
    2 teaspoons orange zest
    salt and pepper, to taste
    2 pounds center-cut salmon fillets

Toss avocado with lemon juice. Add cucumber, cantaloupe, chives, dill and shallots; toss gently and set aside. In a small bowl, whisk together 2 tablespoons olive oil, 2 tablespoons orange juice, 1 teaspoon honey and orange zest. Season with salt and pepper and set aside. Combine remaining 1 tablespoon olive oil, orange juice and honey, making a marinade for fish. Brush over salmon and sprinkle with salt and pepper to taste. Oil grill rack well. Place salmon on grill, flesh side down, 3" from heat source. Cook 10 to 12 minutes over medium-high heat, turning carefully after 4 minutes and brushing with additional marinade. Gently toss avocado salad with dressing. Divide salad evenly among 4 plates. Slice salmon into 4 equal portions and place atop each salad.

Teresa Hayes   **Buena High School, Ventura, CA**

Zero Fat Spinach Salad

Serves: 6   Prep time: 15 minutes

6 - 8 cups fresh spinach OR 1 bag prepared spinach
1 pear, cubed
$^1/_3$ cup craisins (dried cranberries)
$^1/_2$ cup red onion rings
$^1/_3$ cup seasoned rice vinegar
$^1/_3$ cup orange juice

Clean and trim spinach; drain well. Wash pear and cube, leaving skin on. Toss spinach with pear, craisins and red onion rings. Mix rice vinegar and orange juice together and add to salad; toss.

*"This salad is delicious and contains 0 grams of fat.
You can substitute apple for pear if you wish!"*

Sandra Hughes   **Upland High School, Upland, CA**

Side Dishes

Vegetables • Casseroles • Stir Fry

Corn Sesame Saute

Serves: 4   Prep time: 15 minutes

    1 tablespoon butter
    1 clove garlic, minced OR $1/4$ teaspoon garlic powder
    1 tablespoon sesame seeds
    $1/8$ cup green pepper, diced
    $1/2$ teaspoon salt (optional)
    $1/4$ teaspoon basil
    $1/8$ teaspoon pepper
    1 (12 ounce) can whole kernel corn, drained

In a frying pan, saute all ingredients, except corn, until golden and toasted, being careful not to overcook. Stir in drained corn and stir until heated through. Serve hot.

Phyllis Greer   **Vista Verde Middle School, Moreno Valley, CA**

Do Ahead Party Mashed Potatoes

Serves: 10 - 12   Prep time: 15 minutes, Bake: 45 minutes

    10 medium potatoes, parboiled
    2 (3 ounces) packages cream cheese
    1 cup sour cream
    2 teaspoons onion salt
    2 teaspoons garlic salt
    $1/4$ teaspoon pepper
    2 tablespoons butter
    Topping: grated cheddar cheese, paprika

Preheat oven to 350 degrees. Peel potatoes and grate into large bowl. Stir in remaining ingredients; sprinkle cheese and paprika on top. Bake 45 minutes.

NOTE: Can be made ahead and refrigerated up to 24 hours.

"Great make ahead dish for a crowd."

Marjorie Brown   **Cabrillo High School, Lompoc, CA**

Garlic Mashed Potatoes

Serves: 4   Prep time: 30 minutes

    4 new red potatoes (or any variety desired)
    4 tablespoons butter
    1 small can evaporated or regular milk
    fresh garlic, diced, to taste

Scrub potatoes - do not peel. Cut in fairly small pieces (don't dice). Boil potatoes in salted water until tender. Using an electric mixer, mash potatoes. Add butter and milk; mix to desired consistency. Add garlic, starting with a small amount, to taste and mix well.

Sheri Rader   **Chaparral High School, Las Vegas, NV**

Green Bean Casserole

Serves: 6   Prep time: 10 minutes, Bake: 20 minutes

    1 pound mushrooms, diced
    $1/4$ cup onion, diced
    2 tablespoons margarine, butter or olive oil
    $1/4$ cup sharp cheddar cheese, shredded
    2 tablespoons soy sauce
    1 can water chestnuts, sliced
    1 can French cut green beans
    salt and pepper, to taste

Preheat oven to 350 degrees. Saute mushrooms and onion in margarine, butter or olive oil until tender. Stir in cheese until melted. Stir in soy sauce and water chestnuts; simmer 1 to 2 minutes. Place drained green beans in a casserole dish; pour mushroom mixture over beans. Season with salt and pepper. Cover and bake 20 minutes.

Marshawn Porter   **Arroyo Grande High School, Arroyo Grande, CA**

Hopping John

Serves: 4 - 6   Prep time: 10 minutes, Cook 20 minutes

    1 (16 ounce) can black-eyed peas
    1 cup Uncle Ben's converted rice
    $1 1/2$ cups onion, chopped
    $1 1/2$ teaspoons garlic salt
    $1/2$ teaspoon salt
    2 teaspoons chili powder
    $1 1/2$ cups cheddar cheese, shredded

Drain black-eyed peas, reserving liquid. Add water to make $2 1/2$ cups. In a large skillet, combine black-eyed peas, liquid, rice, onions, garlic salt, salt and chili powder. Stir and bring to a boil; cover and simmer 20 minutes. Remove from heat. Sprinkle with cheese. Cover & let stand until liquid is absorbed & cheese melted, about 5 minutes.

Astrid Curfman   **Newcomb Academy, Long Beach, CA**

Italian Green Beans

Serves: 4 - 6 Prep time: 10 minutes, Bake: 15 minutes

3 cups green beans, French cut, drained
1 cup tomato sauce
2 tablespoons onion, chopped
$1/_8$ teaspoon oregano
$1/_8$ teaspoon basil
2 cloves garlic, crushed
nonstick cooking spray, olive oil flavored (optional)
$1/_2$ cup fresh Parmesan cheese, grated

Preheat oven to 350 degrees. In saucepan, combine green beans, tomato sauce, onion, garlic and basil; heat. Pour into casserole dish that has been sprayed with nonstick cooking spray (olive oil spray gives a good flavor). Top with cheese and bake 15 minutes.

Lucille Bell **Quartz Hill High School, Quartz Hill, CA**

Maple Mustard Green Beans

Serves: 8 Prep time: 20 minutes

2 pounds green beans, ends trimmed
2 tablespoons Dijon mustard, coarse grain
3 tablespoons balsamic vinegar
2 tablespoons maple syrup
2 teaspoons olive oil
2 tablespoons green onions, chopped (include tops)
salt and pepper, to taste

In a 4 to 5 quart pan, bring water to a boil over high heat. Add beans and cook, uncovered, until tender crisp, about 5 to 8 minutes; drain and pour into serving bowl. Meanwhile mix mustard with vinegar, maple syrup and oil. Pour over hot beans and mix to coat well. Sprinkle with onion. Season with salt and pepper; serve.

"Great for Thanksgiving and Christmas - good with turkey."

Gage Hewes **South Pasadena High School, So. Pasadena, CA**

Oven Baked Potatoes

Serves: 4 - 5 Prep time: 10 minutes, Bake: 20 minutes

5 to 6 red potatoes
2 tablespoons olive oil, or nonstick olive oil cooking spray
$1/_4$ teaspoon garlic powder
$1/_2$ teaspoon thyme
salt and pepper, to taste

Scrub potatoes; do not peel. Cut into chunks and coat with olive oil. Place on dish or plate and cook in microwave on HIGH 5 minutes. Remove from microwave and coat with remaining spices. Bake in oven at 350 degrees until tender and crunchy, about 20 minutes.

"You will never have any leftovers!"

Maridel Anagnos   **Tokay High School, Lodi, CA**

Potluck Beans

Serves: 6 - 8   Prep time: 10 minutes, Cook: 15 - 20 minutes

4 slices bacon, diced
$1/4$ cup onion, chopped
1 (small) can diced green chiles
1 (16 ounce) can black beans, drained
1 (16 ounce) can kidney beans, drained
1 (16 ounce) can pork and beans
1 (16 ounce) can chili con carne
2 tablespoons catsup
2 tablespoons brown sugar
$1/2$ teaspoon garlic powder

Brown diced bacon and onion together in a large Dutch oven; drain off excess fat. Add remaining ingredients; stir well. Simmer 15 to 20 minutes.

"I had forgotten about the potluck at church until 1 hour before time to leave. I combined these ingredients from my pantry and was ready to go in 30 minutes. The only problem was replicating the recipe for friends!"

Judy Moorc   **Ceres High School, Ceres, CA**

Risoto Milanese

Serves: 4   Prep time: 5 minutes, Cook: 30 minutes

$1/2$ cup butter
1 large onion, chopped
1 $1/2$ cups rice, uncooked
4 $1/4$ cups chicken broth
$1/3$ cup white wine
$1/4$ cup mushrooms, chopped
1 cup Parmesan cheese, grated
salt and pepper, to taste

Melt butter in skillet, saute onion until soft. Add rice, stirring constantly. Add broth and wine. Cover and cook 20 minutes, stirring occasionally. Add mushrooms and cook, uncovered, 10 minutes more. Add Parmesan cheese, salt and pepper to taste and serve immediately.

Simone Clements   **Bret Harte Union High School, Altaville, CA**

Roman Style Green Beans

Serves: 8   Prep time: 30 minutes

    2 pounds fresh green beans, ends trimmed
    4 ounces bacon, cut crosswise into $1/2$" strips
    1 tablespoon olive oil
    $1/2$ teaspoon salt
    $1/4$ cup pine nuts, toasted

In 12" skillet (at least 2" deep) or 5 quart saucepan over high heat, in
1" boiling water, heat green beans to boiling. Reduce heat to low,
simmer 5 to 10 minutes, until beans are tender-crisp; drain. Wipe
skillet dry. In same skillet over medium heat, cook bacon until
golden, stirring frequently. With slotted spoon, remove bacon to
paper towels to drain. In same skillet over medium-high heat, add oil
to bacon drippings. Cook green beans with salt, stirring frequently,
until beans are lightly browned and tender. Spoon onto a warmed
large platter; sprinkle with bacon and toasted pine nuts.

"Beans & bacon can be prepared early then sauteed just before serving."

Linda Hsieh   **Rowland High School, Rowland Heights, CA**

Stir Fry Vegetables

Serves: 3 - 4   Prep time: 10 minutes

    2 tablespoons olive oil
    1 (large) bag frozen vegetables,
    2 tablespoons prepared sun-dried tomatoes with garlic
    salt and pepper, to taste

Heat olive oil over medium-high heat in wok. Add frozen vegetables
and stir-fry until tender. Stir in tomato until heated through. Season
with salt and pepper.

"Quick and easy way to add vegetables to your meal."

Maridel Anagnos   **Tokay High School, Lodi, CA**

Swiss Vegetable Medley

Serves: 6   Prep time: 10 minutes, Microwave: 8 - 10 minutes

    1 (16 ounce) bag frozen vegetable combination, thawed, drained
    1 (10.75 ounce) can cream of chicken soup
    1 cup Swiss cheese, shredded
    $1/3$ cup sour cream
    $1/4$ teaspoon pepper
    1 (2.8 ounce) can French fried onions

In a shallow 1 quart microwave casserole dish, combine vegetables,
soup, $1/2$ cup cheese, sour cream, pepper and $1/2$ can French fried
onions. Microwave, covered, on HIGH 8 to 10 minutes or until
vegetables are done, stirring halfway through cooking. Top with

44

remaining cheese and onions. Microwave, uncovered, 1 minute or until cheese melts. Let stand 5 minutes.

Lori Wilson   **A.B. Miller High School, Fontana, CA**

Szechwan Broccoli

Serves: 4   Prep time: 15 minutes

1 tablespoon soy sauce
1 tablespoon rice vinegar
$1/_2$ teaspoon sugar
1 tablespoon sesame seeds
2 teaspoons vegetable oil
$1/_2$ teaspoon crushed red pepper
$1/_2$ teaspoon ginger
2 cloves garlic, minced
5 cups broccoli, stems and florets, chopped

Combine soy sauce, rice vinegar and sugar in a small bowl; set aside. Heat a large wok over medium heat. Add sesame seeds; cook one minute or until browned. Set aside. Add oil to wok, stir-fry crushed red pepper, ginger and garlic 30 seconds. Add broccoli; stir-fry 1 minute. Add soy sauce mixture; stir well. Cover and cook 2 minutes or until broccoli is crisp-tender. Sprinkle with toasted sesame seeds.

"You can vary this recipe by adding chicken or beef to it."

Carrie Vaughn   **Cypress High School, Cypress, CA**

Baked Goods
Breads • Biscuits • Pancakes

Bitsy Bread

Serves: 10   Prep time: 15 minutes, Bake: 8 - 10 minutes

1 package refrigerator biscuit dough
$1/_3$ cup sugar
1 teaspoon cinnamon
3 tablespoons margarine, melted

Preheat oven to 400 degrees. Line muffin tins with 10 paper liners.
Combine sugar and cinnamon in small bowl; set aside. Separate
biscuits, then tear each biscuit into 3 pieces. Roll each piece into a
ball then roll in melted margarine. Roll in cinnamon sugar mixture
and place 3 in each muffin cup. Bake 8 to 10 minutes, until slightly
browned. Do not let bottoms get too browned.

"This is a hit with my beginning foods students."

Paula Schaefer   **Garside Middle School, Las Vegas, NV**

Blender Popovers

Makes: 12   Prep time: 10 minutes, Bake: 20 minutes

1 cup water
$1/_2$ cup vegetable oil
$1/_2$ teaspoon salt (optional)
1 cup flour
4 large eggs
Toppings: grated cheddar or Parmesan cheese, sliced jalapeños

Preheat oven to 400 degrees. In blender, combine water and oil. Add
salt and flour, blending until well mixed. Add eggs, one at a time, and
blend. Pour into muffin or popover pans, filling about $3/_4$ full. If
desired, sprinkle tops with cheese or jalapeños. Bake 20 minutes or
until golden brown.

"This recipe is compliments of David Will from California Egg Council.
My students love these filled with jelly or whipped cream."

Deborah Weiss   **Ayala High School, Chino Hills, CA**

Caramel Biscuit Ring

Serves: 4   Prep time: 10 minutes, Microwave: 4 $\frac{1}{2}$ minutes

- $\frac{1}{3}$ cup brown sugar
- 3 tablespoons margarine
- 1 tablespoon water
- 1 teaspoon cinnamon
- 1 package refrigerator biscuits

Combine sugar, margarine, water and cinnamon in a round 1 $\frac{1}{2}$ quart microwave casserole dish. Microwave on HIGH 1 $\frac{1}{2}$ minutes; stir well. Cut each biscuit into quarters (kitchen scissors work well!) Add biscuit pieces to the sugar mixture. Stir until they are all coated. Push biscuits away from center of dish; set a 1 cup glass or plastic measuring cup in the center to form a ring. Microwave 3 minutes. Remove hot cup from the center. Put plate upside down on casserole dish. Flip it over and eat immediately! Pull apart with forks for easiest serving.

"This is the #1 favorite recipe of my 8th graders! It's our first cooking lab in class! Caramel biscuit ring is the only recipe my son, Matthew, and his friend, Jeff Dokken, have memorized and cook frequently!"

Gaylen Roe   **Magnolia Junior High School, Chino, CA**

Caramel Rolls

Serves: 4 - 6   Prep time: 10 minutes, Bake: 20 - 25 minutes

- 12 to 15 frozen dinner rolls (unbaked dough)
- 1 (3 $\frac{5}{8}$ ounce) package butterscotch pudding mix, not instant
- $\frac{1}{2}$ cup brown sugar, firmly packed
- $\frac{1}{2}$ cup margarine, melted

Distribute rolls in a single layer in greased 12 cup fluted tube pan. Sprinkle dry pudding mix over rolls. In small bowl, combine brown sugar and margarine; pour over pudding mix. Place in cold oven and let rise overnight. Heat oven to 350 degrees. Bake 20 to 25 minutes. (Rolls will be slightly dark brown on top when centers are thoroughly baked.) Remove from oven. Invert pan onto serving plate. Serve warm.

"I sometimes add chopped nuts."

Eloise Hatfield   **Poston Junior High School, Mesa, AZ**

Chocolate Chip Scones

Serves: 6   Prep time: 15 minutes, Bake: 18 - 20 minutes

- 2 cups flour
- 3 tablespoons sugar
- 1 tablespoon baking powder
- $1/2$ teaspoon salt
- $1/2$ cup vegetable shortening
- $1/2$ cup milk
- 1 large egg
- 1 teaspoon vanilla
- $1/2$ cup chocolate chips

Preheat oven to 425 degrees. Grease a baking sheet. In a large bowl, combine flour and sugar. Cut shortening in with pastry blender until the size of small peas. In a small bowl, combine milk, egg and vanilla; add to dry ingredients along with chocolate chips. Mix with a fork until a soft dough forms. Knead gently 5 to 6 times. Roll or pat dough into a 7" wedges. Cut into wedges. Place scones 1" apart on greased baking sheet. Pierce tops with tines of fork and bake 18 to 20 minutes. Serve warm.

"Great breakfast treat. You can also use fun cookie cutter shapes like hearts to make special shaped scones."

Beverly Ranger   **Carpinteria High School, Carpinteria, CA**

Christmas Morning Scones

Makes: 16   Prep time: 15 minutes, Bake: 15 - 18 minutes

- 1 tablespoon butter (for baking pan)
- 3 cups flour
- $1/2$ cup sugar
- $2 1/2$ teaspoons baking powder
- 1 teaspoon salt
- $1/2$ teaspoon baking soda
- $2/3$ cup butter, room temperature
- 2 tablespoons orange zest, grated
- $3/4$ cup dried cranberries
- $1/2$ cup almonds, chopped
- 1 cup buttermilk
- *Glaze:*
- 2 tablespoons cream
- 2 teaspoons sugar

Preheat oven to 425 degrees. Butter a baking sheet and set aside. In a large bowl mix together flour, sugar, baking powder, salt and baking soda. Using a pastry blender, cut butter into flour. Add orange zest, cranberries and almonds; toss to combine. Stir in buttermilk until mixture is evenly moistened. Place dough on a floured surface and gently knead 10 times. Divide dough in half and pat each half into a

7" circle. Combine cream with sugar and brush each round with glaze. Cut rounds into 8 wedges and place on buttered baking sheet, barely touching. Bake 15 to 18 minutes, until puffy and golden brown.

"Save time by mixing together everything but the buttermilk. Add it just before baking. Experiment with other dried fruits."

Myrna Swearingen   **Corona High School, Corona, CA**

Fiesta Bread

Serves: 9   Prep time: 10 minutes, Bake: 15 - 17 minutes

     2 cups biscuit baking mix
     $2/3$ cup milk
     4 $1/2$ teaspoons chili seasoning mix
     2 tablespoons butter or margarine, melted

Preheat oven to 425 degrees. In a bowl, combine biscuit mix and seasoning mix. Add milk and mix well. Pat into a greased 8" square baking pan. Drizzle with melted butter or margarine. Bake 15 to 17 minutes or until a toothpick inserted in center comes out clean.

"You may substitute any of your favorite seasoning mix, such as Italian or ranch dressing mix, taco seasoning or onion soup mix."

Ellen Pepin   **Moreno Valley High School, Moreno Valley, CA**

German Oven/Apple Pancakes

Serves: 6   Prep time: 10 minutes, Bake: 30 minutes

     $1/4$ cup margarine, melted
     1 $1/2$ cups milk
     $3/4$ cup flour, all purpose or whole wheat
     $1/3$ cup sugar or honey
     3 eggs
     $1/4$ teaspoon salt

Preheat oven to 450 degrees. Melt margarine in a 9" or 10" pie pan. In a blender, mix remaining ingredients and pour into pie pan. Bake 20 minutes; reduce heat to 350 degrees and continue baking for 8 to 10 minutes or until top is browned. Serve warm with apple sauce and cinnamon.

"I often put the ingredients together in a blender the night before and refrigerate it. Then, I just blend and bake when I'm still half awake! This is good leftover, reheated, if you take care not to let it dry out."

Mary Schult   **El Dorado High School, Placentia, CA**

Orva's Coffee Cake

Serves: 6   Prep time: 10 minutes, Bake: 30 minutes

- 2 $^1/_2$ cups flour, sifted
- 1 cup brown sugar
- 1 cup white sugar
- $^3/_4$ cup oil
- 1 teaspoon salt
- 1 tablespoon nutmeg
- 1 egg
- 1 cup sour milk
- 1 teaspoon baking soda
- 1 teaspoon baking powder (if sweet milk is used,
    add 2 $^1/_2$ teaspoons baking powder)

Preheat oven to 375 degrees. Mix the first 6 ingredients and reserve 1 cup for topping. To the remainder, add egg, sour milk, baking soda and baking powder. Stir well and pour into a greased 8" x 8" baking pan. Bake 30 minutes. Cool and serve.

"Grandma's favorite served on Sunday morning with eggs and bacon"

Sonja Tyree   **Ayala High School, Chino Hills, CA**

Oven Baked Sausage Pancakes

Serves: 4   Prep time: 15 minutes, Bake: 15 minutes

- $^1/_2$ pound link sausage
- $^3/_4$ cup milk
- 2 tablespoons oil
- $^3/_4$ cup + 2 tablespoons flour
- 2 teaspoons baking powder
- 2 teaspoons sugar
- $^1/_2$ teaspoon salt
- 2 small eggs

Preheat oven to 450 degrees. Cook sausage as directed on package, set aside. Sift flour, then combine all other dry ingredients and sift again. Beat eggs until light and thick. Stir milk and oil into eggs. Add flour mixture to egg mixture and blend until batter is smooth. Pour batter into an 8" square greased baking pan. Arrange fried sausages on top of batter. Bake 15 minutes, or until slightly golden. Cut into squares and serve immediately.

Jennifer Walker   **Bloomington High School, Bloomington, CA**

Parmesan Twists

Serves: 5 - 6   Prep time: 15 minutes, Bake: 10 - 15 minutes

- 1 loaf frozen bread dough, defrosted
- 3 cloves garlic, minced OR 1 teaspoon garlic powder
- $^1/_3$ cup ranch dressing
- $^1/_3$ to $^1/_2$ cup Parmesan cheese, grated

Defrost frozen bread dough and let rise one hour. Roll dough out onto a floured board into a 12" x 16" rectangle. Add garlic to ranch dressing and spread evenly over bread dough. Sprinkle Parmesan evenly over top. Fold dough in half so that you end up with a 6" x 16" rectangle with dressing mix in center. Carefully cut dough into 1" strips using a butter knife. Lay the strips on an ungreased cookie sheet 1" apart and twist each strip 2 to 3 times. Bake at 375 degrees for 10 to 15 minutes or until golden.

Sue Campbell   **Marsh Junior High School, Chico, CA**

Quick Waffles

Serves: 4   Prep time: 20 minutes

    3 eggs
    1 cup milk
    $1/2$ cup margarine, melted
    1 tablespoon vanilla
    2 cups flour
    $1/2$ teaspoon salt
    1 tablespoon baking powder
    2 teaspoons sugar

Beat eggs in a bowl. Beat in milk, melted margarine and vanilla; mix well. Add flour, salt, baking powder and sugar and mix until well blended. Bake in hot waffle iron and serve with syrup.

Donna Small   **Santana High School, Santee, CA**

Streusel Coffee Cake

Serves: 4 - 6   Prep time: 10 minutes, Bake: 25 minutes

    Coffee Cake:
    1 $1/2$ cups flour
    $3/4$ cup sugar
    1 tablespoon baking powder
    $1/2$ teaspoon salt
    $1/4$ cup shortening
    $3/4$ cup milk
    1 egg
    Topping:
    $1/2$ cup brown sugar
    2 teaspoons cinnamon
    $1/2$ cup nuts, chopped
    2 tablespoons butter, melted

Preheat oven to 375 degrees. Mix together cake ingredients and spread into a greased 8" x 8" pan. Mix together topping ingredients and sprinkle over top of cake. Bake 25 minutes.

Katrina Brighton   **Swainston Middle School, Las Vegas, NV**

Poultry Entrées

Chicken • Turkey • Duck

Apricot Baked Chicken

Serves: 4 - 6　　　　　　　　**Prep time: 10 minutes, Microwave: 20 minutes**

　　2 $^1/_2$ to 3 pounds chicken, cut up
　　$^1/_4$ cup Russian dressing
　　2 tablespoons mayonnaise
　　$^1/_2$ cup apricot preserves
　　$^1/_2$ envelope dry onion soup mix

Arrange chicken pieces in a 2 quart oblong baking dish, placing thickest meaty pieces around edge of dish. Cover with waxed paper and microwave on HIGH 10 minutes; drain excess fat. Mix remaining ingredients and spread over chicken, coating each piece. Cover with waxed paper and microwave on HIGH 10 minutes more. Let stand 5 minutes, covered.

"This recipe is great and easy to prepare."

Olga Sarouhan　　　　　　　　**Edison High School, Huntington Beach, CA**

Blackened Chicken

Serves: 4　　　　　　　　**Prep time: 10 minutes, Cook: 14 minutes**

　　Cajun Mixture:
　　2 $^1/_2$ tablespoons paprika
　　2 tablespoons garlic powder
　　1 tablespoon salt
　　1 tablespoon onion powder
　　1 tablespoon dried thyme
　　1 tablespoon ground red pepper
　　1 tablespoon black pepper
　　4 chicken breast halves
　　nonstick cooking spray

Combine ingredients for Cajun mixture and store in an airtight container. When ready to use, rub chicken breasts with small amount of Cajun mixture. Coat a large heavy skillet with nonstick cooking spray and place over medium-high heat until hot. Add chicken and cook 7 minutes on each side or until done. Remove chicken from skillet and let cool. Cut chicken across grain into thin slices.

*"This is very spicy so go light the first time you use the mix.
This chicken tastes great over salad or pasta. You will only use
a small amount each time, so keep remainder in airtight container."*

Jan Neufeld   Fullerton High School, Fullerton, CA

Braised Chicken and Tomatoes Over Rice
Serves: 4 - 6   Prep time: 30 minutes

    4 pounds chicken, cut into 8 to 12 pieces
    fresh ground pepper
    3 tablespoons virgin olive oil
    3 cloves garlic, minced
    $1/2$ cup dry white wine
    $1/4$ cup balsamic vinegar
    5 large plum tomatoes, seeded, coarsely chopped
    2 tablespoons fresh rosemary, snipped
    $1/2$ teaspoon mustard seed
    2 to 3 cups rice, cooked

Season chicken with freshly ground pepper. Heat oil in large skillet
and sear chicken on all sides, turning occasionally for about 10
minutes. Transfer to a large platter and keep warm. Drain off all but
3 tablespoons pan drippings. Saute garlic in pan drippings for about 1
minute at medium heat. Turn up heat and add wine. Simmer
vigorously until reduced by half. Add vinegar, tomatoes, rosemary and
chicken. Cover and simmer gently 10 to 12 minutes. NOTE: If you
start the rice cooking before you begin chicken, both will be done at
the same time!

*"Serve immediately over the rice.
Fresh garlic and fresh rosemary are a must in this recipe."*

Sandra Massey   Mountain View High School, El Monte, CA

Cashew Chicken
Serves: 4   Prep time: 20 minutes

    $3/4$ pound boneless, skinless chicken breasts, cut into $1/2$" cubes
    1 $1/2$ tablespoons cornstarch
    2 tablespoons dry sherry or sake
    1 $1/2$ tablespoons soy sauce
    5 tablespoons oil, divided
    1 $1/2$ green peppers, cut into $1/2$" squares
    6 water chestnuts, diced
    $1/4$ pound fresh mushrooms, sliced
    salt, to taste
    2 to 3 tablespoons hoisin sauce
    $1/4$ cup cashews, roasted
    2 cups rice, cooked

Marinate chicken in mixture of cornstarch, sherry and soy sauce. Put 2 tablespoons oil in wok over medium heat. Add green peppers, water chestnuts, mushrooms and salt. Stir-fry 2 to 3 minutes. Remove with slotted spoon. Add remaining 3 tablespoons oil and heat over high heat. Add chicken and stir- fry 2 to 3 minutes, until chicken turns white. Stir in hoisin sauce. Return cooked vegetables to wok and stir-fry 2 minutes more. Add cashews, stir to heat through, 1 to 2 minutes.

Sue Hope　　　　　　　　　**Lompoc High School, Lompoc, CA**

Champagne Chicken
Serves: 4　　　　　　　Prep time: 15 minutes, Cook: 15 - 30 minutes

    4 whole chicken breasts, deboned, skinned
    $1/_3$ cup flour
    1 teaspoon salt
    $1/_8$ teaspoon white pepper
    4 tablespoons butter
    2 tablespoons olive oil
    1 $1/_2$ cups champagne
    1 cup whipping cream
    $1/_2$ cup mushrooms, sauteed
    2 cups rice, cooked

Preheat oven to 200 degrees. Flatten chicken breasts and coat with flour seasoned with salt and pepper. Heat butter and olive oil in skillet until hot. Sauté chicken breasts until browned, about 5 minutes. Add champagne and simmer 15 to 30 minutes. After chicken is cooked, remove from skillet and place in baking dish. Place chicken in oven to keep warm. Add whipping cream to butter and oil that chicken was cooked in; stir and cook until thickened. Pour sauce over chicken, add mushrooms and serve over hot cooked rice.

Peggy Herndon　　　　**Central Valley High School, Shasta Lake City, CA**

Chicken & Broccoli
Serves: 4 - 5　　　　　　　Prep time: 10 minutes, Bake: 30 minutes

    1 (1 pound) package frozen broccoli spears
    3 chicken breast halves, cooked
    1 can cream of chicken soup
    $1/_2$ cup Miracle Whip
    $1/_2$ teaspoon lemon juice
    $1/_4$ teaspoon curry powder
    $1/_2$ cup cheddar cheese, shredded
    1 small package almonds, sliced

Preheat oven to 350 degrees. Cook broccoli to desired doneness; drain. Cut chicken breasts in half. Arrange chicken and broccoli in bottom of a 9" x 9" baking dish. Mix together soup, Miracle Whip, lemon juice and curry powder. Pour over chicken and broccoli. Top with shredded cheese and almonds. Bake 30 minutes.

Carol Fleming   Rancho Cucamonga High School, Rancho Cucamonga, CA

Chicken Cacciatore

Serves: 4   Prep time: 25 minutes

    3 tablespoons flour
    1 teaspoon dried oregano
    $1/2$ teaspoon salt (optional)
    $1/4$ teaspoon pepper
    4 boneless, skinless chicken breast halves
    1 $1/2$ tablespoons olive or vegetable oil
    1 medium onion, chopped
    2 cloves garlic, minced
    1 (16 ounce) can stewed tomatoes, undrained
    1 large green bell pepper, chopped
    2 cups rice or noodles, cooked

Combine flour and seasonings in plastic bag. Add chicken breasts, one at a time, shaking to coat. In skillet, heat oil over medium heat. Add chicken; cook 3 to 4 minutes or until golden brown. Turn, add onion and garlic. Continue 4 to 5 minutes or until onion is crisp and tender. Add tomatoes, green pepper; cook, uncovered, about 8 minutes until chicken is no longer pink inside and sauce thickened, turn chicken after 4 minutes. Serve over hot, cooked rice or noodles.

Gale Hooper   Casa Roble High School, Orangevale, CA

Chicken Caesar Pasta

Serves: 4 - 6   Prep time: 30 minutes, Chill: several hours

    1 pound penne or other pasta
    1 tablespoon butter
    $1/4$ cup red wine vinegar
    1 $1/2$ pounds boneless, skinless chicken breasts, cooked, cubed
    1 large tomato, diced
    $1/4$ teaspoon salt
    $1/4$ teaspoon pepper
    $1/2$ cup Parmesan cheese, grated
    $3/4$ cup bottled Caesar dressing

Prepare pasta according to package directions; drain and toss with butter and vinegar. Add chicken, tomato, Parmesan, salt and pepper. Stir in Caesar dressing and toss. Refrigerate several hours or overnight to allow flavors to blend.

"Great summer supper."

Nanci Burkhart   Hueneme High School, Oxnard, CA

Chicken Cordon Bleu
Serves: 4 - 6   Prep time: 30 minutes

    4 boneless, skinless chicken breast halves
    $1/_4$ teaspoon salt
    $1/_8$ teaspoon pepper
    2 tablespoons butter or margarine
    1 $1/_2$ cups water
    $1/_4$ cup white wine
    1 package herb and butter rice mix
    4 slices ham
    4 slices Swiss cheese
    1 tablespoon parsley, finely chopped

Season chicken breasts with salt and pepper. In large skillet over medium-high heat, melt butter or margarine; brown chicken on both sides. Remove from pan and set aside. In same pan, heat water and wine, bringing to a boil. Add rice and contents of seasoning packet; reduce heat. Top rice mixture with browned chicken breasts, layering ham slices on top. Cover and simmer 15 minutes. Top chicken with cheese slices. Cover and simmer 5 minutes longer, until liquid is absorbed and cheese is melted. Garnish with parsley.

Ginger Raven   **Chico Junior High School, Chico, CA**

Chicken Dijon
Serves: 4   Prep time: 30 minutes

    3 tablespoons butter
    4 boneless, skinless chicken breast halves
    2 tablespoons flour
    1 cup chicken broth
    $1/_2$ cup light cream
    2 tablespoons Dijon mustard
    Garnish: 2 tomatoes, cut in wedges, 2 tablespoons fresh parsley, minced

Melt butter in large skillet. Add chicken breasts and cook until done and lightly browned, about 20 minutes. Remove chicken to warm serving platter. Stir flour into drippings in skillet and cook 1 minute. Add the chicken broth and light cream. Cook and stir until sauce bubbles and thickens. Stir in mustard. Return chicken to skillet; cover and heat 10 minutes. Garnish with tomatoes and sprinkle with parsley.

"This is delicious, especially when served with rice and a green salad."

Terri Gravison   **Las Plumas High School, Oroville, CA**

56

Chicken Fajitas

Serves: 4   Prep time: 20 minutes

2 tablespoons oil
1 tablespoon worcestershire sauce
1 tablespoon soy sauce
1 tablespoon vinegar
dash ground red pepper
1 teaspoon chili powder
1 clove garlic, minced
$1/_2$ onion, cut into long, thin strips
$1/_2$ bell pepper, cut into long, thin strips
2 chicken breast halves, boned, cut into cubes
$1/_2$ lemon
4 flour tortillas, soft taco size
Garnish: avocado, salsa, sour cream

In large frying pan, heat oil with worcestershire sauce, soy sauce, vinegar, ground red pepper, and chili powder. Add garlic, onion and bell pepper and cook until onion is transparent. Add chicken and cook 5 to 8 minutes or until meat is no longer pink on the inside. When ready to serve, squeeze lemon over fajitas and serve on warm tortillas. Garnish as desired.

"My students love this recipe - even the vegetables!"

Cari Sheridan   **Grace Yokley Middle School, Ontario, CA**

Chicken Fingers With Honey Sauce

Serves: 3 - 4   Prep time: 20 minutes, Bake: 11 - 13 minutes

12 ounces boneless, skinless chicken breast halves
2 egg whites, beaten
$1/_4$ cup + 1 tablespoon honey, divided
2 cups cornflakes, crushed
$1/_4$ teaspoon pepper
4 teaspoons Dijon mustard
$1/_4$ teaspoon garlic powder

Preheat oven to 450 degrees. Cut chicken into strips $3/_4$" wide, 3" long. Combine beaten egg whites with 1 tablespoon honey. Place crushed cornflakes and pepper in shallow dish; mix. Dip chicken into egg whites, then roll in corkflakes. Place in single layer on ungreased cookie sheet. Bake 11 to 13 minutes. Meanwhile, mix remaining honey with Dijon mustard and garlic powder and drizzle over chicken or use as a dipping sauce.

"This recipe comes from my sister-in-law, Annie, of Prescott, Arizona."

Joan Goodell   **Eldorado High School, Las Vegas, NV**

Chicken Nuggets

Serves: 4   Prep time: 10 minutes, Bake: 12 - 15 minutes

   1 cup cornflakes, crushed
   $1/2$ cup Parmesan cheese, grated
   $1/2$ teaspoon salt
   $1/4$ teaspoon pepper
   $1/8$ teaspoon garlic powder
   $1/4$ cup ranch dressing, prepared
   1 pound boneless, skinless chicken breast , cut into 1" cubes
   Additional Ranch Dressing

Preheat oven to 400 degrees. In a shallow bowl, combine first 5
ingredients. Place $1/4$ cup ranch dressing in another bowl, Toss
chicken cubes in dressing, then roll in cornflake mixture. Place in a
greased 11" x 7" x 2" baking pan. Bake, uncovered, 12 to 15 minutes,
or until juices run clear. Serve with additional dressing for dipping.

Shirley Marshman   **West Middle School, Downey, CA**

Chicken Parmesan with Potatoes

Serves: 4 - 6   Prep time: 10 minutes, Cook: 15 - 20 minutes

   $1/4$ cup Parmesan cheese, grated
   $1/4$ cup fine bread crumbs
   1 tablespoons parsley, minced
   2 tablespoon margarine or butter
   3 to 4 boneless, skinless chicken breast halves
   1 to 2 cans whole potatoes, reserve $1/2$ can liquid

Using a ziploc bag, combine Parmesan cheese with bread crumbs and
parsley. Coat chicken a few pieces at a time in bag. Melt margarine or
butter in frying pan. Place chicken in pan and brown both sides.
Place whole potatoes in pan with chicken. Sprinkle remaining
Parmesan cheese/bread crumb mixture all around top of chicken and
potatoes. Add liquid from potatoes into pan. Cover and simmer 15 to
20 minutes.

"I give this recipe out more than anything else I cook.
It always gets rave reviews. It's almost impossible to kill it!"

Georgia Frawley   **Eisenhower High School, Rialto, CA**

Chicken Parmesana

Serves: 6 Prep time: 10 minutes, Cook: 20 - 25 minutes

1 egg, beaten
6 boneless, skinless chicken breast halves
3 tablespoons olive oil
$1/2$ cup bread crumbs
$1/4$ cup flour
$1/2$ cup + 2 tablespoons Parmesan cheese, grated, divided
1 teaspoon garlic powder
1 jar pasta sauce
$1/2$ to $3/4$ cup white wine
1 cup mozzarella cheese, grated

Place beaten egg in bowl and moisten chicken breasts. In flat or pie plate, combine bread crumbs with flour, 2 tablespoons Parmesan cheese and garlic powder. Coat chicken with mixture and saute in olive oil until browned on both sides. Spoon 2 to 3 spoonfuls of pasta sauce on top of each breast. Pour wine into pan; cover and simmer 15 to 20 minutes. Combine remaining Parmesan with grated mozzarella cheese and top each breast; simmer 5 minutes more.

"Jamie brings her sorority sisters home for this one!"

Gail McAuley **Lincoln High School, Stockton, CA**

Chicken Piccata

Serves: 4 Prep time: 25 minutes

4 boneless, skinless chicken breast halves
2 tablespoons flour
2 tablespoons oil
2 tablespoons butter
1 clove garlic, minced
$1/2$ cup chicken broth
$1/4$ cup white wine
2 tablespoons lemon juice
1 tablespoon capers
1 tablespoon parsley, chopped

Pound chicken breasts to $1/4$" thickness. Dredge in flour. Heat butter and oil in skillet over medium heat. Brown breasts on both sides, about 2 minutes each side. Add garlic, broth, wine and lemon juice. Cover and simmer 10 minutes. Remove chicken from pan. Add capers and parsley, cooking until thickened. Return chicken to sauce, serve.

"This is quick and delicious!"

Pat Hufnagel **Esperanza High School, Anaheim, CA**

Chicken Sour Cream Enchiladas

Serves: 4   Prep time: 15 minutes, Microwave: 5 - 8 minutes

1 cup sour cream
1 cup cream of chicken soup
2 cups chicken, cooked, shredded
$1/3$ cup green chiles, diced
$1/4$ teaspoon cumin
8 corn tortillas
2 green onions, diced
1 cup cheddar cheese, grated
oil

In a small bowl, combine sour cream and chicken soup, divide in half and set half aside for topping. Combine remaining half with chicken, green chiles and cumin; blend well. Heat oil. Soften tortillas in hot oil, drain lightly on paper towels, then spoon chicken mixture into each tortilla and roll to close. Place rolled tortillas, folded side down into a greased baking dish. Top with remaining sour cream, green onions and grated cheese. Microwave on MEDIUM 5 to 8 minutes or until heated through, or bake at 350 degrees for 25 minutes.

Jan Hirth   **Saddleback High School, Santa Ana, CA**

Chicken Spindi

Serves: 6   Prep time: 10 minutes, Cook: 15 - 20 minutes

4 boneless, skinless chicken breast halves, cubed
1 red onion, cut into cubes
1 can chunk pineapple, drained
wooden or metal skewers
$1/2$ cup butter
$1/2$ cup white wine
$1/2$ teaspoon garlic
$1/2$ teaspoon fresh rosemary

Alternate chicken, red onion and pineapple on skewers until all ingredients are used. Broil 15 to 20 minutes, or until chicken is cooked. Meanwhile, in a skillet, melt butter. Stir in white wine, garlic and rosemary. Cook on medium-high heat until sauce slightly reduces, stirring occasionally. Pour sauce over chicken skewers or serve on the side.

"These can also be cooked on the barbecue!"

Alicia Pucci   **Kenilworth Junior High School, Petaluma, CA**

Chicken Taco Bake

Serves: 4   Prep time: 10 minutes, Bake: 20 minutes

- 1 pound chicken, cut into cubes
- 1 (10.75 ounce) Campbell's tomato soup
- 1 cup salsa
- $1/2$ cup milk
- 6 flour tortillas, cut into 1" pieces
- 1 cup cheddar cheese, shredded
- 1 can refried beans

Preheat oven to 400 degrees. In skillet over medium-high heat, cook chicken until browned and juices run clear; pour off fat. Add soup, salsa, milk, refried beans, tortillas and half of the cheese. Spoon into a 2 quart shallow baking dish. Cover and bake about 20 minutes, until hot. Sprinkle with remaining cheese and serve.

"It is quick and easy. My family loves it!"

Anne Cornell   **Turlock High School, Turlock, CA**

Chicken Teriyaki Strips

Serves: 4   Prep time: 15 minutes, Cook: 20 minutes

- 4 boneless, skinless chicken breast halves
- $1/4$ cup soy sauce
- $1/4$ cup rice vinegar
- $1/4$ cup oil
- 1 clove garlic, minced
- 2 tablespoons brown sugar
- 1 tablespoon catsup

Cut chicken into strips. Combine remaining ingredients and marinate chicken strips 10 minutes or longer (even overnight). Remove from marinade and place chicken strips on foil lined 9" x 13" pan. Broil for 10 minutes, then turn over and broil and additional 10 minutes.

"Can be garnished with toasted sesame seeds or fresh chopped cilantro."

Anne Silveira   **Shasta High School, Redding, CA**

Chicken With A Twist

Serves: 4   Prep time: 20 minutes

- 1 $1/2$ cups dry corkscrew macaroni
- 1 tablespoon oil (optional)
- $1/2$ large green pepper, chopped (about 1 cup)
- $1/2$ (10.75 ounce) can Campbell's cheddar cheese soup
- 2 tablespoons milk
- $1/4$ cup + 2 tablespoons Pace picante sauce
- $1/4$ teaspoon garlic powder or 2 cloves garlic, minced
- $1/4$ to $1/2$ cup chicken, cooked, cubed

In large saucepan, cook macaroni in boiling water until done, about 8 to 10 minutes, stirring occasionally. (You may wish to add 1 tablespoon oil to keep macaroni from sticking.) Add green pepper for last 4 minutes of cooking time. Drain in colander. In same saucepan, mix soup, milk, picante sauce, garlic, macaroni with green pepper and chicken. Over low heat, heat through. NOTE: Substitute 1 (10 ounce) can Swanson Chunk White Chicken, drained, for cooked chicken.

"The students in my Foods class enjoy this simple dish."

Janet Griffith   **Norco High School, Norco, CA**

Clifford's Marinated Chicken
Serves: 6 - 8   Prep time: 30 minutes, Marinate: 6 hours
  6 to 8 boneless, skinless chicken breast halves
  1 (16 ounce) bottle Bernstein's Italian dressing
  1 (16 ounce) jar salsa (or more, if desired)

Place frozen or thawed chicken breasts in a 13" x 9" pan. Cover chicken with dressing and salsa, then seal pan with plastic wrap. Marinate 3 to 6 hours. Grill chicken breasts on barbecue 10 to 20 minutes, until juices run clear when poked with fork.

"This is a great summer time dinner or anytime, because there is so little preparation and mess and the chicken is moist and delicious. My best friend in Utah gave me this recipe."

Karen Frey   **Hesperia High School, Hesperia, CA**

Corn 'n Salsa Chicken Pockets
Serves: 4   Prep time: 10 minutes, Bake: 18 - 22 minutes
  4 skinless, boneless chicken breast halves
  $1/2$ cup thick and chunky salsa
  2 cups corn, drained (preferably Mexicorn)
  $1/2$ cup fresh tomato, chopped
  1 cup cheddar cheese, shredded

Preheat oven to 450 degrees. Tear 4 sheets aluminum foil about 12" x 18". Center chicken breast half on each foil sheet. Spoon salsa over chicken; add vegetables on top. Wrap and seal foil to form four packets. Bake 18 to 22 minutes. When serving, spoon vegetables over chicken and sprinkle with cheese.

"I cook rice at the same time. This is quick, easy and very tasty."

Doris Oitzman   **Victor Valley High School, Victorville, CA**

Creamed Turkey With Cranberry Whirls

Serves: 8   Prep time: 20 minutes, Bake: 20 - 25 minutes

1 package frozen peas
2 (10.75 ounce) cans condensed cream of chicken soup
3 cups chicken or turkey, cooked, cut up
1 cup milk, divided
2 cups Bisquick baking mix
1 can cranberry sauce

Preheat oven to 425 degrees. Cook peas in a 1 $^{1}/_{2}$ quart saucepan or microwave as directed on package; drain. Stir in soup, cooked chicken or turkey and $^{3}/_{4}$ cup milk. Pour into ungreased 1 $^{1}/_{2}$ quart casserole dish. Heat to boiling in microwave. Mix Bisquick with $^{1}/_{4}$ cup milk until soft dough forms; beat vigorously 30 seconds. Turn onto cloth covered surface, well floured with baking mix; knead 10 times. Roll dough into 6" x 9" rectangle; spread with cranberry sauce. Roll up, beginning at 9" side. Cut into $^{3}/_{4}$" slices. Arrange slices on hot turkey mixture and bake until cranberry whirls are golden brown, 20 to 25 minutes.

"This is a good way to use leftover turkey at holiday time. On the day the turkey is cooked, divide into bite-sized pieces and freeze in 3 cup portions. This is even better the next day."

Mary Schult   **El Dorado High School, Placentia, CA**

Creamy Chicken Fettuccini Alfredo

Serves: 4   Prep time: 15 minutes

8 ounces cream cheese, cut into cubes
$^{3}/_{4}$ cup Parmesan cheese, grated
$^{1}/_{2}$ cup margarine
$^{1}/_{4}$ cup milk
1 can cooked chicken
1 cup broccoli florets, steamed (optional)
8 ounces fettuccini noodles, cooked

In a large saucepan, stir together cream cheese, Parmesan, milk and margarine over low heat until smooth. Stir in chicken and broccoli; heat through. Serve over warm fettuccini noodles.

"A nice alternative to macaroni and cheese. Nutritious and delicious."

Linda Stroup   **Virgin Valley High School, Mesquite, NV**

Curry Seasoning for Chicken and Pork

Prep time: 10 minutes

2 tablespoons flour
1 tablespoon Lawry's seasoned salt
1 $^1/_2$ teaspoons Spice Island curry powder
$^3/_4$ teaspoon paprika
$^1/_2$ teaspoon ground black pepper
$^1/_2$ teaspoon allspice
$^1/_2$ teaspoon dehydrated orange peel

Mix all ingredients together and store in a spice bottle with a shaker top so it's ready to use any time. This recipe can easily be doubled or tripled. *Use as follows:* shake curry mixture on meat and brown in skillet with canola oil; cook until desired doneness. May be used on canned chicken (cook 10 minutes); chicken tenders, (cook 20 minutes); chicken breasts (20 to 30 minutes); pork chops (30 minutes +).

"While in college, I volunteered to assist a Southern California Gas Company home economist with a food demonstration. I have shared this recipe with many friends and relatives."

Joyce Doig   **Ranchero Middle School, Hesperia, CA**

Easy Italian Chicken Bake

Serves: 4   Prep time: 25 minutes, Bake: 5 minutes

4 boneless, skinless chicken breast halves
2 tablespoons oil
1 (1 pound, 8 ounce) jar Ragu Chicken Tonight Cacciatore Sauce
1 (3 ounce) can mushrooms, sliced
5 ounces mozzarella cheese, sliced
2 cups pasta or rice, cooked

Cut chicken breasts into pieces; brown in hot oil. Drain off any remaining oil. Add sauce and mushrooms and simmer 20 minutes. Place mixture in a shallow baking dish and cover with sliced cheese. Bake, uncovered, at 350 degrees until cheese melts. Serve over hot cooked pasta or rice.

"This variation of chicken cacciatore is very tasty and easy to prepare."

Wanda Shelton   **Newport Harbor High School, Newport Beach, CA**

Southwest Caesar Salad
10 min. of preparation.
Page 36

**Pasta in Tomato
Cream Sauce**
15 min. of preparation.
Page 122

San Antonio Beef Stew
30 min. of preparation.
Page 90

**Honey Teriyaki
Mini Meatloaves**
30 min. of preparation.
Page 83

Fusilli With Sun-Dried Tomato Cream
Serves: 4   Prep time: 30 minutes

$1/_4$ cup olive oil
4 cloves garlic, chopped
$1/_2$ large red onion, finely diced
1 pound boneless chicken breast halves, cooked, seasoned, diced
$1/_4$ pound bacon, cooked crisp, diced
$1/_4$ cup basil, chopped
2 ounces sun-dried tomatoes, chopped, reconstituted in water
$3/_4$ cup dry white wine
1 $3/_4$ cups heavy whipping cream
3 ounces Parmesan cheese, grated
salt and pepper, to taste
2 pounds fusilli noodles, cooked

Heat oil in skillet; add garlic and onion, saute. Add chicken, bacon, basil and sun-dried tomatoes; saute 10 minutes more. Add wine and simmer until liquid is reduced by half. Add cream and Parmesan cheese. Cook until sauce is reduced to a creamy consistency. Season with salt and pepper. Add to cooked pasta in large bowl and toss.

"This is not a diet dish, but I'd rather treat myself with this delicious dish than to eat a piece of candy on a special occasion."

Jan Schulenburg   **Irvine High School, Irvine, CA**

Gourmet Chicken
Serves: 7 - 8   Prep time: 10 minutes, Bake: 30 - 45 minutes

8 boneless, chicken breast halves
8 slices sharp cheddar cheese
2 cans cream of chicken soup
$1/_2$ cup milk
2 tablespoons mayonnaise
1 package Stove Top stuffing, with seasoning packet
$1/_2$ to 1 cup margarine, melted

Preheat oven to 350 degrees. Place chicken breasts in 9" x 13" baking dish. Top each breast with a slice of cheese. In a bowl, mix together soup, milk and mayonnaise; pour over chicken. Mix together stuffing with seasoning packet and sprinkle over chicken and soup mixture. Drizzle with melted margarine. Bake 30 to 45 minutes, or until chicken is tender. NOTE: Swiss cheese can be substituted for cheddar and applesauce can be substituted for milk.

"This recipe is really gourmet, and so quick to prepare. Always a big hit!"

Roberta Hawkes   **A.B. Miller High School, Fontana, CA**

Grandma's Chicken Casserole

Serves: 6 - 8   Prep time: 10 minutes, Bake: 15 - 20 minutes

1 pound chicken, cooked, shredded
2 cans cream of chicken soup
2 cups milk
2 cans refrigerator biscuits
salt and pepper, to taste

Grease 9" x 13" pan. Heat oven to 425 degrees. Spread shredded chicken on bottom of pan. Mix soup with milk and pour over chicken. Place biscuits on top to cover. Salt and pepper, to taste. Bake 10 minutes, or until biscuits are browned, turn biscuits and bake 5 to 10 minutes more, or until biscuits are browned.

"Frozen vegetables can be added and lowfat soup and milk can be substituted."

Carrie Salisbury   **Monte Vista High School, Spring Valley, CA**

Honey Chicken

Serves: 4   Prep time: 10 minutes, Bake: 30 - 45 minutes

$1/3$ cup butter, melted
$1/2$ cup honey
$1/4$ cup prepared mustard
1 tablespoon curry powder
1 teaspoon chili powder
4 chicken breast halves, or 1 whole frying chicken, cut up

Heat oven to 375 degrees. In baking pan, combine melted butter, honey, mustard, curry powder and chili powder; stir well. Roll pieces of chicken in sauce to coat well on all sides. Bake 30 to 45 minutes, basting often.

Sharon McKenzie   **Ray Kroc Middle School, San Diego, CA**

Jiffy Chicken Stew
Serves: 4   Prep time: 25 minutes

   4 boneless, skinless chicken breast halves
   2 tablespoons vegetable oil (divided)
   1 (medium) onion, chopped
   3 ribs celery, coarsely chopped
   6 carrots, peeled, thinly sliced
   1 cup fresh mushrooms, sliced
   1 (14.5 ounce) can tomatoes, peeled, cut up, undrained
   $1/_3$ cup dry white wine (optional)
   $1/_2$ teaspoon garlic, minced
   $1/_2$ teaspoon rosemary
   1 teaspoon salt
   pepper, to taste
   1 tablespoon flour
   2 tablespoons cold water
   1 (14.5 ounce) can whole new potatoes, drained
   1 (9 ounce) package frozen green beans, French-cut, thawed

Cut chicken into $3/_4$" cubes. In 10" or 12" skillet, heat 1 tablespoon oil over high heat until hot. Add chicken and stir-fry quickly over high heat until it turns white, 3 to 4 minutes; remove to plate. Add remaining tablespoon oil to skillet and heat. Stir in onion, celery, carrots and mushrooms. Cook over medium heat, stirring frequently, until vegetables are tender-crisp, about 5 minutes. Mix in tomatoes with their liquid, white wine, garlic, rosemary, salt and pepper. Heat to boiling. Dissolve flour in cold water and stir into stew. Heat to boiling. Add potatoes and green beans. Reduce heat to medium-low and simmer 5 minutes. Stir in chicken and simmer 2 minutes longer.

*"This is delicious, fast and easy. I serve it with
a green salad and crisp French bread."*

Sally Reimers   **Sinaloa Middle School, Simi Valley, CA**

Julie's Barbecued Chicken Pizza
Serves: 4 - 6   Prep time: 10 minutes, Bake: 10 - 15 minutes

   3 chicken breasts, cooked and cubed
   1 cup barbecue sauce, hickory or honey
   $1/_2$ bunch cilantro, chopped
   3 tablespoons honey
   1 teaspoon molasses
   $1/_3$ cup brown sugar
   $1/_2$ red onion, sliced
   1 cup smoked gouda cheese, shredded
   1 baked pizza crust (Boboli)

Preheat oven to 425 degrees. Place the first six ingredients in a saucepan and bring to a boil, stirring occasionally. Pour over pizza crust. Top with onion slices and shredded cheese. Bake 10 to 15 minutes, until cheese melts.

"Serve this with a tossed green salad. The ingredients can be prepared ahead of time and poured over pizza crust at the last minute."

Bonnie Landin　　　　　**Garden Grove High School, Garden Grove, CA**

Mexican Chicken Casserole
Serves: 6　　　　　Prep time: 10 minutes, Microwave: 8 - 12 minutes

2 (10.75 ounce) cans cream of mushroom soup
$1/_2$ cup water
6 - 8 corn or flour tortillas
6 green onions, chopped
2 cups chicken, cooked, chopped
2 cups cheddar or Monterey jack cheese, shredded
1 (4 ounce) can jalapeños, diced
1 (2.25 ounce) can ripe olives, sliced

Mix together soup, water and onions to form sauce. Using a 9" x 12" pan, cover bottom of pan with thin layer of sauce. Top with tortillas, covering bottom. Pour another layer of sauce, layer of green onions, chicken, cheese, jalapeños and olives. Continue layering until all ingredients are used, ending with generous layer of cheese on top. Garnish with any remaining olives. Microwave on 70% power 8 to 12 minutes, until heated through. NOTE: May also be baked at 350 degrees 25 to 30 minutes.

"If all ingredients are ready, it takes 10 minutes to be assembled Serve with salad and vegetables."

Liz Thornburg　　　　　**Selma High School, Selma, CA**

One Pan Potatoes & Chicken
Serves: 4　　　　　Prep time: 25 minutes

4 medium potatoes, cut in wedges
1 pound chicken, boned, skinned, cut in strips
1 to 2 tablespoons oil
$1/_2$ cup green onions, sliced
$1/_4$ cup teriyaki sauce

Microwave potato wedges on HIGH 8 to 10 minutes. While potatoes cook, heat oil over high heat in large skillet. Brown chicken, about 5 minutes. Add potatoes to skillet and saute until lightly browned. Add green onions and teriyaki sauce; heat through.

Penny Niadna　　　　　**Golden West High School, Visalia, CA**

Orange Cashew Chicken

Serves: 4   Prep time: 20 minutes, Cook: 10 minutes

- 1 tablespoon margarine
- 4 boneless, skinless chicken breasts, about $1/4$ pound each
  cut into bite-sized pieces
- $1/2$ cup celery, sliced diagonally
- $1/4$ cup onion, thinly sliced
- 1 (10.75 ounce) can cream of chicken soup
- $1/2$ cup orange juice
- dash pepper
- dash nutmeg
- dash cloves
- $1/4$ cup cashews, chopped
- 1 orange, peeled, sliced
- 1 to 2 tablespoons honey (optional)

Melt margarine in frying pan. Cook chicken breasts until lightly browned and juices run clear when poked with fork, about 4 to 5 minutes. Remove from pan and keep warm. Saute celery and onion 3 to 5 minutes, until tender-crisp. Add soup, orange juice, spices and cashews. Stir to combine, then cover and simmer over medium-low heat 5 minutes. Add chicken, orange slices, and honey, if desired. Cover and simmer 5 minutes more. Serve over rice.

Ann Hardman   **Livermore High School, Livermore, CA**

Penne With Sausage & Broccoli

Serves: 4   Prep time: 30 minutes

- 1 pound penne pasta
- 3 cups broccoli florets
- 4 cloves garlic, minced
- 12 ounces lowfat turkey or chicken sausage, casing removed
- $1/2$ cup fat free chicken or vegetable broth
- $1/2$ cup Parmesan cheese, grated
- 1 tablespoon olive oil
- 2 tablespoons balsamic vinegar
- ground black pepper

Cook pasta in a large pot of boiling water for 8 minutes. Add broccoli and cook 3 minutes or until both are tender. Drain and place in a large bowl. Coat a nonstick skillet with nonstick cooking spray and place over medium heat. Add garlic and cook 1 minute. Crumble sausage into skillet. Cook 5 minutes or until browned. Pour over pasta. Add the broth, Parmesan cheese, oil and vinegar to pasta. Toss to mix. Season with pepper.

Vicki Giannetti   **Foothill High School, Sacramento, CA**

Pineapple Chicken

Serves: 6   Prep time: 10 minutes, Bake: 30 - 45 minutes

6 chicken breasts
salt and pepper, to taste
1 package Lipton onion soup mix
1 (16 ounce) jar apricot pineapple preserves
1 bottle Russian dressing
1 can chunk pineapple, drained

Preheat oven to 350 degrees. Line large baking dish with foil and arrange chicken breasts, skin side up. Season with salt and pepper. In separate bowl, mix remaining ingredients and pour over chicken. Bake, uncovered, 30 to 45 minutes.

Carmen Leonard   **Mission Viejo High School, Mission Viejo, CA**

Quick Chicken Stew

Serves: 4   Prep time: 15 minutes, Bake: 20 minutes

3 tablespoons olive oil
2 carrots, sliced
1 yellow onion, diced
2 boneless, skinless chicken breast halves, cut into cubes
1 cup frozen peas
2 (14 ounce) cans chicken broth
salt and pepper, to taste
$1/_4$ teaspoon cumin
$1/_4$ teaspoon garlic powder
$1/_4$ teaspoon poultry seasoning
3 tablespoons flour
3 tablespoons butter

Preheat oven to 350 degrees. In large nonstick skillet, heat 1 tablespoon olive oil over medium heat. Saute carrots and onion until tender, about 5 minutes. Remove with slotted spoon and place in 2 quart casserole; set aside. Add 2 tablespoons oil to skillet and brown chicken with spices; set aside. In saucepan, melt butter; stir in flour making a roux. Gradually add chicken broth and simmer until thickened. Add frozen peas and browned chicken to vegetables in casserole. Stir in thickened sauce and bake 20 minutes.

"Created by my husband one winter night. Serve with popovers."

Darlene Lupul   **Tokay High School, Tokay, CA**

Ranchero Wrap-Ups

Serves: 4   Prep time: 10 minutes

     2 cups chicken or beef, cooked, shredded
     1 (14.5 ounce) can Del Monte Diced Tomatoes with Garlic & Onion
     1 cup salsa
     1 (15.25 ounce) can Del Monte Fiesta Corn, drained
     1 (4 ounce) can diced green chiles, drained
     $1/_2$ cup green onions, sliced
     4 flour tortillas
     1 cup Monterey jack or cheddar cheese, shredded

Combine meat, tomatoes, salsa, corn, chiles and onions in skillet; cook 5 minutes, stirring occasionally. Wrap tortillas in plastic wrap and heat in microwave oven 1 minute on HIGH until hot. Spoon $1/_4$ of chicken mixture down center of each tortilla. Top with $1/_4$ cup cheese. Roll up and serve.

Del Monte Foods   **San Francisco, CA**

Roasted Bell Pepper Chicken Fettuccini

Serves: 4   Prep time: 30 minutes

     2 boneless, skinless chicken breasts
     1 to 2 tablespoons olive oil
     1 to 2 cloves garlic, minced
     $1/_2$ cup roasted red bell pepper, prepared (in jar)
     salt and pepper, to taste
     8 ounces fresh fettuccini noodles
     2 cups prepared creamy red bell pepper sauce (Costco brand)

Cut chicken into $1/_2$" cubes and saute in olive oil until opaque. Add garlic and roasted bell peppers. Season with salt and pepper, to taste. Add creamy red bell pepper sauce and heat over low heat. Meanwhile, cook fettuccini in boiling salted water until al dente (firm to the tooth but not mushy). Drain and add to creamy chicken mixture. Serve hot.

"This is so fast and easy and especially delicious if you love roasted bell peppers! It will be a big hit with family and friends."

Sue Zallar   **Capistrano Valley High School, Mission Viejo, CA**

Rosemary Orange Chicken

Serves: 4   Prep time: 25 minutes

     4 boneless, skinless chicken breast halves
     2 tablespoons olive oil or butter
     1 (medium) shallot, thinly sliced
     juice of 1 orange
     juice of $1/_2$ lime
     2 teaspoons dried rosemary or 1 tablespoon fresh

In medium skillet, saute chicken in olive oil or butter until brown on both sides. Remove from pan and set aside. Add shallot to pan and saute until translucent. Add juice, a little at a time. Let mixture reduce about 4 minutes. Add rosemary. Place chicken in sauce and simmer 5 minutes, turning several times to absorb liquid on both sides.

"Makes the house smell good too!"

Karen Giles   **Cordova High School, Rancho Cordova, CA**

Saucy Orange Chicken
Serves: 3   **Prep time: 30 minutes**

    3 chicken drumsticks, skinned (if desired)
    3 chicken thighs, skinned (if desired)
    1 tablespoon oil
    $1/4$ cup water
    Sauce:
    $3/4$ cup orange juice
    2 tablespoons brown sugar
    2 teaspoons cornstarch
    $1/4$ teaspoon salt
    dash pepper
    dash nutmeg
    Garnish: orange slices (optional)

In medium skillet over medium high heat, brown chicken in oil. Reduce heat; add water. Cover and simmer 15 to 20 minutes or until chicken is fork tender and juices run clear. Drain, if necessary. Transfer chicken to serving platter and keep warm. In small bowl, combine all sauce ingredients except orange slices; blend well. Pour into skillet and cook until mixture thickens and boils, stirring constantly. Pour sauce over chicken; garnish with orange slices, if desired.

"I like to serve this over rice, and it's ready in 30 minutes!"

Jeri Drake Lane   **Canyon Springs High School, Moreno Valley, CA**

Shrimpy Chicken Roll-Ups
Serves: 4   **Prep time: 10 minutes, Bake: 20 minutes**

    2 cups pink baby shrimp, frozen
    1 can cream of chicken soup
    1 to 2 tablespoons dill
    3 green onions, chopped
    4 chicken breast fillets, pounded flat
    1 egg, beaten
    bread crumbs

Preheat oven to 450 degrees. Combine shrimp, chicken soup, dill and green onions; set aside. Flatten chicken between two pieces of waxed paper. Dip chicken breasts in beaten egg; fill with $1/2$ cup filling and roll up, securing with toothpick. Roll in bread crumbs and bake 20 minutes.

"I've impressed guests with this recipe, and it's so easy!"

Jan Schulenburg   **Irvine High School, Irvine, CA**

Special Chicken Filling

Serves: 8 - 10   Prep time: 20 minutes

    4 cups chicken, cooked, cubed
    4 tablespoons lemon juice
    1 teaspoon salt
    2 cups celery, thinly sliced
    2 cups green grapes, seedless, sliced if preferred
    4 eggs, hard cooked, chopped
    1 cup mayonnaise
    $1/2$ cup almonds, sliced

Mix all ingredients together in order listed. Spread on sliced croissants for sandwiches or serve on a bed of lettuce as a salad.

"This recipe has become a favorite for all occasions.
Our last serving was on mini-croissants for my daughter's bridal tea."

Gerry Henderson   **Temple City High School, Temple City, CA**

Spicy Wild Duck

Serves: 4   Prep time: 20 minutes, Cook: 15 minutes

    3 duck breasts
    2 tablespoons cider vinegar
    2 tablespoons lime juice
    1 $1/2$ teaspoons chili powder
    3 tablespoons oil
    2 $1/2$ cups onion, chopped
    1 (7 ounce) can green chilies, diced
    1 $1/2$ tablespoons ginger, minced
    1 $1/2$ tablespoons cilantro, minced
    1 $1/2$ teaspoons salt
    $1/2$ teaspoon tumeric
    2 cloves garlic, minced
    1 (28 ounce) can diced tomatoes
    $3/4$ cup water
    2 cups rice, cooked
    Garnish: chopped cilantro, mango chutney

Cut duck breasts into cubes. Marinate in vinegar, lime juice and chili powder for 10 minutes. Remove from marinade and brown in oil over high heat. Add onion, chilies, spices and garlic; cook until onion is transparent. Add tomatoes and water and simmer on medium to high

73

heat 15 minutes. Serve in soup bowls over cooked rice. Garnish with cilantro and mango chutney.

*"For extra punch, add 2 to 3 finely chopped jalapeños
Wild Mallard or other large duck is best."*

Kevil Pelton   **Nevada Union High School, Grass Valley, CA**

Sweet 'n Spicy Chicken
Serves: 4   Prep time: 15 minutes

1 pound boneless, skinless chicken breasts, cut into $1/_2$" cubes
3 tablespoons taco seasoning
1 to 2 tablespoons vegetable oil
1 (11 ounce) jar chunky salsa
$1/_2$ cup peach preserves
2 cups rice, cooked

Place chicken in a large ziploc bag; add taco seasoning and toss to coat. In a skillet, brown chicken in oil. Combine salsa with preserves; stir into skillet and bring to a boil. Reduce heat; cover and simmer 2 to 3 minutes, or until meat juices run clear. Serve over hot rice.

Ellen Pepin   **Moreno Valley High School, Moreno Valley, CA**

Swiss Chicken Cutlets
Serves: 4   Prep time: 30 minutes

2 slices Swiss cheese
4 boneless, skinless chicken breast halves, pounded $1/_4$" thick
2 tablespoons all-purpose flour
$1/_2$ teaspoon black pepper
1 tablespoon unsalted butter
$1/_2$ cup chicken broth
$1/_4$ cup dry white wine
$1/_4$ teaspoon dried oregano
$1/_4$ teaspoon dried basil

Cut each cheese slice in half; place 1 half on top of each piece of chicken. Starting with short end of breast, roll up, jelly roll style and tie securely with string. On waxed paper, combine flour and pepper; mix well. Add chicken and toss gently to coat. In large nonstick skillet, melt butter over medium heat. Add breasts; cook, turning frequently until golden, about 3 minutes. Add broth, wine, dried oregano and basil to skillet. Increase heat, bringing to a boil. Reduce heat to medium-low; simmer until chicken is cooked through and sauce is slightly thickened, about 10 to 12 minutes. Place on serving plate. Remove string.

Donna Fippin   **Bret Harte Union High School, Altaville, CA**

White Chicken Chili

Serves: 6   Prep time: 20 minutes, Cook: 10 minutes

- 3 boneless, skinless chicken breast halves
- 2 tablespoons butter
- 2 stalks celery, diced
- 2 carrots, diced
- 1 small onion, diced
- 1 (12 ounce) can chicken broth
- 2 (14 ounce) cans great northern beans
- 1 (14 ounce) can diced tomatoes
- 2 tablespoons chili powder
- salt and pepper, to taste

Dice chicken breast into $1/2$" cubes. Saute in butter. Add celery, carrots, onion and chicken broth; cook until tender. Drain beans and add to vegetable chicken mixture. Add tomatoes, chili powder and seasoning. Simmer 10 minutes.

"Nice change from traditional chili. Tastes great with corn bread."

Nancy Hunyadi   **Fullerton High School, Fullerton, CA**

Beef Entrées
Stew • Chili • Meatloaf

Beef Stroganoff by Ava
Serves: 4   Prep time: 10 minutes, Cook: 25 minutes

    1 pound beef round, cut into cubes
    1 tablespoon oil (optional)
    1 can cream of mushroom soup
    $1/_2$ cup sour cream
    $1/_4$ cup onion, chopped
    $1/_4$ cup mushrooms, sliced
    1 beef bouillon cube
    1 tablespoon worcestershire sauce
    $1/_4$ cup red wine
    12 ounces egg noodles, cooked

Brown beef in large skillet (you may use 1 tablespoon oil, but it's not necessary). Add onions and cook until soft. Stir in soup, sour cream, mushrooms, bouillon and worcestershire sauce. Simmer on medium-low heat, covered, for 20 minutes. Stir in wine and simmer 5 minutes more. Serve over hot, cooked noodles.

Ava Smalley   **La Puente High School, La Puente, CA**

Beef Stroganoff by Tami
Serves: 4   Prep time: 25 minutes

    1 medium onion, chopped
    $1/_2$ cup mushrooms, sliced
    1 $1/_2$ teaspoons ginger root, grated
    1 tablespoon cooking oil
    1 pound lean ground beef or sirloin steak, thinly sliced across grain
    1 (10.5 ounce) can cream of mushroom soup
    $1/_2$ cup sour cream
    salt and pepper, to taste
    2 cups hot cooked rice or noodles

Saute onion, mushrooms and ginger in oil until onion is transparent. In a separate pan, cook beef until browned; drain excess fat, then add onion, mushrooms and ginger. Blend in soup and heat thoroughly. Add sour cream and blend well. Heat gently to a serving temperature and remove from heat. Add salt and pepper to taste. Serve over hot rice or noodles.

"This is one of my favorite 'quick' recipes. I just cook it up and add a vegetable accompaniment."

Tami Fuhrmann-Cramer **Kelseyville High School, Kelseyville, CA**

Beefy Biscuit Cups
Serves: 8   Prep time: 15 minutes, Bake: 15 - 17 minutes

1 pound ground beef
1 (14 ounce) jar spaghetti sauce
2 (8 ounce) packages refrigerated biscuits
1 cup cheddar cheese, shredded

Preheat oven to 375 degrees. Brown ground beef in skillet; drain. Stir in spaghetti sauce; cook over medium heat 5 to 10 minutes or until heated through. Press biscuits onto bottom and up sides of greased muffin cups. Spoon 2 tablespoonfuls meat mixture into center of each cup. Bake 15 to 17 minutes or until golden brown. Sprinkle with cheese; bake 3 minutes longer or until cheese is melted.

"A great recipe to prepare in a foods class when time is short!"

Carole Delap   **Golden West High School, Visalia, CA**

Big Chili Mac
Serves: 6   Prep time: 10 minutes

1 package macaroni and cheese, prepared
1 can chili

Combine prepared macaroni and cheese with a can of chili in saucepan; heat and serve.

Linda Vincent   **Turlock High School, Turlock, CA**

Chili and Rice Roll-Ups
Serves: 3 - 6   Prep time: 15 minutes

1 pound ground beef
1 (15 ounce) can chili
1/2 cup water
1 cup Minute Rice
6 flour tortillas
Garnish: grated cheddar cheese, diced tomato, chopped green onion

Brown ground beef and drain excess fat. In a medium saucepan, bring chili and water to a boil. Stir in rice. Cover and cook on low for 5 minutes or until rice is done. Stir beef into beans and rice. Heat tortillas slightly in microwave and spoon bean mixture into each tortilla. Garnish as desired. Roll up sides of tortilla to enclose filling.

"This is a favorite...from my 4 year old to my high school Foods Class kids!"

Julie Hampton   **Gresham High School, Gresham, OR**

Chili Bean Enchiladas

Serves: 6   Prep time: 20 minutes, Bake: 20 minutes

    3 cans chili beans (or equal amount of homemade)
    2 eggs
    2 1/2 cups water
    1 1/2 cups flour
    1 1/2 cups cornmeal
    1 teaspoon salt
    2 cups cheddar cheese, grated

Heat beans in saucepan. Beat eggs and water in a bowl; add dry ingredients and mix well. Using a lightly oiled skillet, cook batter "crepe style". As each crepe is done, fill with 2 to 3 tablespoons beans and and place seam side down in a 9" x 13" pan. Repeat with remaining batter. Pour remaining beans over enchiladas. Top with cheese and bake at 325 degrees for 20 minutes.

"A quick dinner that pleases. Thanks Aunt Dotty."

Jean Hanson   **Red Bluff High School, Red Bluff, CA**

Chili Ravioli Bake

Serves: 4   Prep time: 5 minutes, Bake: 10 - 15 minutes

    1 can ravioli
    1 can corn, drained
    1 can chili, no beans
    1/2 cup cheese, grated
    1 cup corn chips, crushed

Preheat oven to 350 degrees. In a casserole dish, layer the ravioli, corn and chili. Top with grated cheese and crushed corn chips. Bake in oven 10 to 15 minutes, until hot and bubbly.

"Very fast to make - great for potlucks. I always get comments on this, and it's so easy! Enjoy!"

Brenda Hardt   **Taft Union High School, Taft, CA**

Chinese Pepper Steak

Serves: 4   Prep time: 30 minutes

    1 pound beef, cut into 1/4" strips
    1 tablespoon onion
    1/2 onion, thinly sliced
    1/2 cup celery, thinly sliced
    1 large green pepper, thinly sliced
    1 cup beef consomme
    salt and pepper, to taste
    1 tablespoon cornstarch
    1/4 cup water
    1 tablespoon soy sauce
    2 cups rice, cooked

In large skillet, brown sliced beef in oil over medium-high heat. Add onion, celery, green pepper, consomme; simmer, covered 20 minutes. Salt and pepper to taste. In a small bowl combine cornstarch with water and soy sauce. Add to beef mixture and simmer 5 minutes more. Add a little more water, if too thick. Serve over hot cooked rice.

Pat Johnson   **Iron Horse Middle School, San Ramon, CA**

Crunchy Cheeseroni
Serves: 4 - 6   Prep time: 10 minutes, Bake: 30 minutes

    2 cups macaroni
    1 pound ground beef
    1 can cream of mushroom soup
    1 can tomato soup
    1 green pepper, diced
    1 can Durkee French fried onion rings (divided)
    4 ounces cheddar cheese, shredded (divided)

Preheat oven to 350 degrees. Cook macaroni in boiling salted water until al dente, about 10 minutes. Meanwhile, brown ground beef in skillet; drain excess fat. Drain cooked macaroni. In a bowl, combine soups. Stir in diced green pepper, cooked ground beef and macaroni. Pour half of the mixture in a 9" x 13" pan. Layer with $1/2$ of the onion rings and half of the cheese. Place remaining macaroni mixture on top. Sprinkle remaining cheese on top and bake 25 minutes. Sprinkle remaining $1/2$ onion rings on top and bake 5 minutes longer.

Alison Tichenor   **Rancho High School, N. Las Vegas, NV**

Crustless Pizza
Serves: 4   Prep time: 10 minutes, Bake: 20 minutes

    1 pound ground beef
    $2/3$ cup evaporated milk
    $1/4$ cup bread crumbs
    $1/$ teaspoon garlic salt
    $1/3$ cup catsup
    1 (2 to 3 ounce) can mushrooms
    1 cup cheddar cheese, shredded

Preheat oven to 450 degrees. Combine ground beef, evaporated milk, bread crumbs and garlic salt. Pat into a pie pan. Top with catsup, mushrooms and cheese. Bake 20 minutes.

Bonnie Shrock   **Kearny High School, San Diego, CA**

Easy Rice Bowls

Serves: 4 - 6   Prep time: 30 minutes

    1 (8 ounce) rib eye steak
    1 teaspoon dark sesame oil, divided
    1 cup green onion, sliced into 1" pieces
    2 cups cabbage, shredded
    asparagus, bok choy or broccoli
    2 packages baked ramen noodle soup
    1 $\frac{1}{2}$ cups water
    1 tablespoon low sodium soy sauce
    4 cups rice, cooked

Trim fat from meat; cut diagonally across grain into thin slices. Heat $\frac{1}{2}$ teaspoon oil in large nonstick skillet over medium heat. Stir fry steak until desired doneness; remove from pan and keep warm. Add remaining $\frac{1}{2}$ teaspoon oil to skillet. Add vegetables and stir-fry until tender; remove from pan and keep warm. Remove noodles from packages; save 1 seasoning packet for another recipe. Add water and 1 seasoning packet to pan; bring to a boil. Break noodles in half; add to pan and cook until liquid is absorbed. Stir in meat and vegetables. Serve over rice.

> *"This is from 'Cooking Light', 10/98. We use steak, chicken or a couple of pork chops. My sons help chop vegetables. We often add red bell pepper for color."*

Jeri Lundy   **Grossmont High School, La Mesa, CA**

Easy Taco Pie

Serves: 6   Prep time: 20 minutes, Bake: 3 minutes

    25 to 30 round corn tortilla chips
    $\frac{1}{4}$ onion, chopped
    1 tablespoon oil
    1 pound ground meat
    1 teaspoon chili powder
    1 package taco seasoning mix
    $\frac{1}{2}$ cup catsup
    $\frac{1}{2}$ cup cheddar cheese, grated
    Garnish: shredded lettuce, diced tomatoes, sour cream

Preheat oven to 350 degrees. Line the bottom and sides of a 9" pie plate with tortilla chips. In a frying pan, saute onion in oil. Add meat and chili powder, cooking until well done. Add taco seasoning and catsup; mix well. Spoon mixture over tortilla chips, sprinkle with cheese and bake until cheese is melted, about 3 minutes. To serve, cut into wedges and scoop pie onto individual plates. Garnish as desired.

"I make this in a vegetarian version using nonfat refried beans layered first, and Green Giant Garden Burger for Recipes (in place of meat). My daughter still doesn't know she's eating meatless!"

Marion S. Anderson   **A.G. Currie Middle School, Tustin, CA**

Enchilada Casserole

Serves: 6   Prep time: 15 minutes, Bake: 30 minutes

    1 pound ground beef
    $1/_4$ cup onion, chopped
    $1/_2$ teaspoon garlic
    $1/_4$ teaspoon black pepper
    1 small can green chiles, diced
    1 can nacho jalapeño cheese soup
    1 can cream of mushroom soup
    9 corn tortillas
    $1/_2$ cup cheddar cheese, shredded

Preheat oven to 350 degrees. Brown ground beef; drain off fat. Add onion, garlic, pepper and green chiles. Cook 2 to 3 minutes. Pour both soups into meat mixture and stir until mixed. In a 9" x 13" casserole, layer, beginning with 3 corn tortillas, add $1/_3$ of the meat/soup mixture and continue until all ingredients are used. Sprinkle shredded cheese across top and bake 30 minutes.

"Serve this dish with a fresh green salad and you're ready for company!"

Debra Jamison   **Basic High School, Henderson, NV**

Fajitas

Serves: 2 - 4   Prep time: 20 minutes, Cook: 5 minutes

    1 pound beef skirt steak, flank steak or top round steak, cut $1/_2$" thick
    juice of 2 to 3 limes
    1 $1/_2$ teaspoons garlic salt
    $1/_2$ teaspoon pepper
    4 flour tortillas, warmed
    Garnish: chopped tomato, diced onion, guacamole, sour cream

Trim excess fat and gristle from steak. Pound steak to $1/_4$" thickness. Place in ziploc bag and sprinkle both sides with lime juice, garlic salt and pepper. Seal bag and marinate in refrigerate 6 to 8 hours, or overnight. Drain marinade; discard. Broil steak over medium hot coals or broil 2 to 3 minutes on each side. Carve across grain into thin slices. Serve in warmed tortillas and garnish as desired.

"This is a delicious lunch or dinner treat!"

Joan Wayland   **O.W. Holmes Junior High School, Davis, CA**

Ground Beef Skillet

Serves: 4   Prep time: 20 minutes, Bake: 10 - 15 minutes

    1 pound ground beef
    3 cups uncooked medium egg noodles
    1 envelope onion soup mix
    8 ounces tomato sauce
    2 cups water
    Garnish: green pepper rings

Cook beef on medium heat until it loses its red color; stir while
cooking. Drain off fat. With heat turned OFF, layer cooked beef in
bottom of pan. Place noodles in a layer over meat. Sprinkle with soup
mix. Pour tomato sauce and water over all. DO NOT STIR! Push
noodles into liquid with back of spoon. Cover pan and cook on high
heat until steam appears around edge of cover. Lower heat to
medium-low and cook 10 to 15 minutes. Check often to prevent
burning. Stir skillet ingredients and place in serving bowl. Garnish
with green pepper rings.

"This quick and tasty dish has been a home and classroom favorite for years!"

Chris Borden   **Orange Glen High School, Escondido, CA**

Hamburger and Tater Casserole

Serves: 6   Prep time: 10 minutes, Bake: 20 minutes

    1 pound hamburger
    1 onion, chopped
    1 (16 ounce) package tater tots
    1 can cream of mushroom soup
    1 cup cheddar cheese, shredded

Preheat oven to 350 degrees. Brown hamburger with chopped onion;
drain excess fat. Combine hamburger and onion with remaining
ingredients and pour into large casserole dish. Bake 20 minutes.

"My family always chooses this casserole over any others."

Faye Nielsen   **Rosemead High School, Rosemead, CA**

Honey Teriyaki Mini Meat Loaves & Noodle Toss

Serves: 6   Prep time: 30 minutes

1 $1/_2$ pounds lean ground beef
$1/_2$ cup dry plain bread crumbs
$3/_4$ cup K.C. Masterpiece Honey Teriyaki Barbecue Sauce, divided
1 egg
$1/_4$ teaspoon pepper
Noodle Toss:
1 (16 ounce) package frozen Oriental vegetable mixture
2 cups water
2 (3 ounce) packages Oriental flavored instant ramen noodles
$1/_4$ cup green onion, thinly sliced
3 tablespoons K.C. Masterpiece Honey Teriyaki Barbecue Sauce

Preheat oven to 400 degrees. In large bowl, combine ground beef, bread crumbs, $1/_2$ cup barbecue sauce, egg and pepper, mixing lightly but thoroughly. Place approximately $1/_4$ cup beef mixture into each of 12 medium (2 $1/_2$" diameter) muffin cups, pressing lightly; spread remaining $1/_4$ cup barbecue sauce over tops. Bake 20 minutes or until centers are no longer pink. Meanwhile, prepare *Noodle Toss:* In 10" skillet, combine vegetables, water, noodles (broken into several pieces) and seasoning packet from one package noodles (reserve remaining seasoning packet for another use); bring to a boil. Reduce heat to low, simmer 2 to 3 $1/_2$ minutes or until noodles are tender, stirring occasionally. Stir in green onions and barbecue sauce. Remove meat loaves from pan; serve with noodles.

National Cattleman's Beef Association   Chicago, IL

"In A Stew" Stew

Serves: 4   Prep time: 5 minutes, Cook: 10 - 12 minutes

2 (16 ounce) cans beef stew
1 (15 ounce) can stewed tomatoes
1 (12 ounce) can whole kernel corn, drained
1 (4 ounce) can mushrooms, sliced, drained

Turn beef stew into a deep saucepan. Add tomatoes, corn and mushrooms. Bring to a boil; cover and simmer 10 to 12 minutes. Serve in deep bowls.

"Add a small salad, muffins and you're ready for the hungry kids."

Margaret McLeod   **Nogales High School, La Puente, CA**

Joe's Ground Beef Special

Serves: 4 - 6   Prep time: 20 minutes

    1 ¹/₂ pounds ground beef
    2 tablespoons olive or vegetable oil
    2 (medium) onions, chopped
    2 cloves garlic, minced
    ¹/₂ pound mushrooms, sliced
    1 ¹/₂ teaspoons salt
    ¹/₄ teaspoon nutmeg
    ¹/₄ teaspoon pepper
    ¹/₄ teaspoon oregano
    1 (10 ounce) package frozen spinach, chopped OR
        ¹/₂ pound fresh spinach, washed and chopped
    4 to 6 eggs, beaten

Brown ground beef in oil in large skillet. Add onion, garlic and mushrooms, Cook until onion is soft. Stir in seasonings and spinach; cook about 5 minutes. Add eggs and cook until eggs are set. Serve and enjoy.

"Easy to vary the amounts of the ingredients to accommodate your taste or amount of ingredients on hand."

Nicole Hansen   **Reedley High School, Reedley, CA**

Macaroni Goulash

Serves: 4- 6   Prep time: 15 minutes, Cook: 15 - 20 minutes

    1 pound lean ground beef
    1 medium onion, sliced
    1 medium green pepper, chopped
    2 cups tomato sauce
    2 cups water
    2 cups macaroni, uncooked
    2 tablespoons sugar
    ³/₄ teaspoon salt
    ³/₄ teaspoon sweet basil

In Dutch oven, brown ground beef; drain excess fat. Add onion and green pepper; continue frying until tender. Add remaining ingredients, cover and simmer 15 to 20 minutes, stirring occasionally, until macaroni is tender.

"Quick, easy and good!"

Cathy Miller   **Montclair High School, Montclair, CA**

Microwave Meat Loaf

Serves: 6   Prep time: 5 minutes, Microwave: 10 minutes

- 1 $1/2$ pounds ground beef
- 1 (8 ounce) can tomato sauce
- 1 egg, slightly beaten
- 1 cup rolled oats
- 1 tablespoon minced onion
- $1/8$ teaspoon garlic, minced
- 1 $1/2$ teaspoons salt
- $1/4$ teaspoon pepper
- $1/3$ cup catsup
- 1 teaspoon worcestershire sauce
- 1 tablespoon dark brown sugar
- 1 tablespoon prepared mustard

In a large bowl, combine first 8 ingredients and put into glass loaf pan. Cook in microwave on HIGH power 4 to 5 minutes. Combine last 4 ingredients and pour over partially cooked mixture. Return to microwave and cook on HIGH another 4 to 5 minutes. Let stand 4 to 5 minutes to finish cooking. Drain excess grease and serve.

"This is a good, quick recipe, given to me by my good friend and neighbor, Kitty."

Joanne Montoy   **Esperanza High School, Anaheim, CA**

Mom's Almost Homemade Chili

Serves: 6 - 10   Prep time: 15 minutes, Cook: 10 minutes

- 2 pounds ground round
- $1/2$ onion, chopped
- 1 (30 ounce) can stewed tomatoes (optional)
- 2 (30 ounce) cans Hunt's chili beans
- 2 (30 ounce) cans water
- 1 (16 ounce) XLNT chili con carne brick (found in the deli section)
- *Garnish:* grated cheese, diced onion, sour cream, diced tomatoes, sliced black olives

Brown ground beef with onion, leaving meat in bigger chunks; drain excess fat. Add stewed tomatoes, chili beans, and water. Remove layer of fat from brick of chili con carne and discard. Add brick to chili and break up into smaller pieces. Heat to simmer, about 10 minutes, or until brick has dissolved completely. NOTE: Before starting, make a box of Marie Callender's corn bread mix and by the time the corn bread is done, so is the chili!

"This is one of my family's favorites, especially on a cool evening when the family is on the go. Great in summer, too. Spread the chili on a bed of flour tortillas and then layer with our favorite toppings, just like a pizza.
It's a cool way to eat a hot meal, but you'll need a fork instead of a spoon!"

Barbara Allen   **Ayala High School, Chino Hills, CA**

Mom's Stroganoff

Serves: 4 - 6   Prep time: 25 minutes

    1 pound ground beef or turkey
    $1/4$ cup onion, chopped
    1 clove garlic, minced
    1 can cream of mushroom soup
    $1/2$ cup milk
    2 tablespoons sherry (optional)
    $1/2$ cup sour cream
    salt and pepper, to taste
    8 ounces wide noodles, cooked
    Garnish: chopped parsley

Lightly brown meat in large skillet; drain excess fat. Add onion and garlic and continue to brown. While stirring, add in soup and milk; heat well. Reduce heat to low and stir in sherry, then sour cream. Season to taste with salt and pepper. Serve over hot noodles. Sprinkle with parsley.

"This is a recipe that I grew up with. It's easy and kids love it too!"

Deanna Lee   **Marina High School, Huntington Beach, CA**

Nacho Casserole

Serves: 8 - 10   Prep time: 10 minutes, Bake: 20 minutes

    2 pounds ground beef
    $1/2$ onion, chopped
    1 can cream of chicken soup
    1 can cream of mushroom soup
    1 $1/2$ cups picante sauce
    1 (4 ounce) can diced green chiles
    1 (medium sized) bag tortilla chips
    $3/4$ pound cheddar cheese, grated
    1 (4 ounce) can black olives, sliced

Preheat oven to 350 degrees. Brown beef with onion; drain off fat. Add soups, sauce and chiles; mix well. In 13" x 9" baking pan, layer $1/2$ of the tortillas chips, $1/2$ of the meat mixture, $1/2$ of the cheese and $1/2$ of the olives. Repeat layers. Bake 20 minutes, until bubbly.

"Students love this! A salad can be prepared while the casserole is in the oven for a complete meal."

Cheryl McDaniels   **Green Valley High School, Henderson, NV**

Peppercorn Beef

Serves: 4　　　　　　　　　　　　　　　　Prep time: 15 minutes

1 London broil, sliced $^3/_8$" thick
1 tablespoon butter or olive oil
3 cubes beef bouillon or 1 heaping teaspoon granules
2 tablespoons flour
2 to 3 cups water
1 to 2 tablespoons green peppercorns

Brown beef in butter or olive oil over medium heat in frying pan, turning constantly, until done and browned on outside but still pink inside. Remove meat to a casserole dish with lid. Add bouillon to frying pan with a little water until dissolved. Add flour to make roux, stirring to make smooth and remove any lumps. Add water, a little at a time until desired gravy thickness is achieved. Add peppercorns and simmer until they are are tender. Pour gravy over beef in casserole and keep warm in 300 degree oven until ready to serve.

Karen Giles　　　　　　　　**Cordova High School, Rancho Cordova, CA**

Picadillo

Serves: 3 - 4　　　　　　　　　　　　　　　Prep time: 20 minutes

2 tablespoons cooking oil
2 large cloves garlic, minced
1 large onion, coarsely chopped
1 teaspoon ground cumin
salt and pepper, to taste
1 pound ground beef
$^1/_3$ cup dry white wine
2 large ripe tomatoes, chopped
$^1/_2$ cup dark or light raisins
1 cup hot water
$^1/_3$ cup pimento-stuffed olives, sliced into thirds
1 green pepper, seeded, chopped into $^1/_2$" squares
1 cup rice, cooked

In oil, fry garlic and onion 5 minutes, stirring frequently. Add seasonings, meat, wine and stir again; cook until meat is no longer pink. Add tomatoes, raisins and olives; stir. Add green pepper and cook only long enough for it to get thoroughly hot (it should remain crisp and bright green). Serve over cooked rice.

"This is what Cubans do with ground beef instead of preparing hamburgers. There are many versions of it, but this one is the most authentic. We love picadillo's very unique and special flavor!"

Helen Lievre　　　　　　　　**La Canada High School, La Canada, CA**

Pizza Hero Sandwich

Serves: 6   Prep time: 15 minutes, Bake: 15 minutes

    1 tablespoon vegetable oil
    1 (medium) onion, chopped
    1 pound lean ground beef
    2 (8 ounce) cans tomato sauce
    $1/_2$ teaspoon dried oregano
    $1/_2$ teaspoon dried basil
    $1/_4$ teaspoon dried rosemary
    $1/_2$ teaspoon salt
    $1/_4$ teaspoon pepper
    1 loaf Italian or French bread, about 18" long
    2 cups mozzarella cheese, shredded (about 8 ounces)

Preheat oven to 350 degrees. Heat oil in large skillet. Add onion and beef and cook 5 minutes over moderate heat until onion is soft and beef is browned. Drain off excess fat. Add tomato sauce and spices; stir until blended. Cut bread in half lengthwise. Scoop out center of each half, leaving a shell 1" thick. (Save scooped out center for bread crumbs for another use.) Place half of beef mixture in each half loaf. Sprinkle with cheese. Place on ungreased baking sheet and bake 15 minutes. Cut into 6 portions. Serve hot.

Linda Paskins   **Cordova High School, Rancho Cordova, CA**

Pizza Pockets

Serves: 4 - 6   Prep time: 20 minutes, Bake: 8 - 10 minutes

    1 package refrigerator biscuits
    $1/_2$ pound ground turkey or beef
    2 to 4 tablespoons onion, finely chopped
    $1/_4$ teaspoon garlic salt
    dash pepper
    $1/_2$ cup pizza sauce
    $1/_2$ cup cheese, grated

Preheat oven to 400 degrees. Separate biscuits. Roll each one on a floured surface into a 5" circle. Brown meat and onion in skillet; drain off fat. Stir in garlic salt and pepper. Add pizza sauce. Place a heaping tablespoonful of meat mixture on each biscuit circle; sprinkle with cheese. Fold in half and seal edges with fork. Bake 8 to 10 minutes, until browned. NOTE: This recipe can be changed in so many ways: you can make your own biscuits... use chicken or pepperoni instead of turkey... add other seasonings or ingredients like mushrooms, peppers or olives...salsa can be substituted for the pizza sauce. Fry the pizza pockets instead of baking them!

"My students love this recipe!"

Kathy Sandoz   **Mesa Junior High School, Mesa, AZ**

Quick & Easy Chili

Serves: 4   Prep time: 15 minutes, Cook: 15 minutes

- $1/2$ cup onion, chopped
- 1 pound ground beef
- $1/2$ teaspoon garlic powder
- $1/2$ teaspoon chili powder
- salt, to taste
- $1/2$ teaspoon pepper
- 1 (15 ounce) can diced tomatoes
- 1 large can pinto beans

Saute onion with ground beef until browned; drain excess fat. Add spices, tomatoes and beans. Simmer 15 minutes; serve.

"Wonderful chili, not too spicy! Lowfat, great over rice.
Makes great leftovers. A favorite of my students!"

Rhonda Pratt   **Joe Walker Middle School, Quartz Hill, CA**

Quick & Easy Chili Beans

Serves: 6   Prep time: 25 minutes

- 2 pounds lean ground beef
- 2 medium yellow onions, chopped
- 1 medium green pepper, chopped
- 3 tablespoons chili powder
- 2 teaspoons oregano
- 2 teaspoons garlic, minced
- $1/4$ teaspoon hot pepper sauce
- 2 (16 ounce) cans kidney beans
- 1 (16 ounce) can stewed tomatoes
- 1 (small) can diced green chiles
- 1 can tomato soup

Cook beef over medium heat, until browned; drain excess fat. Add onion, bell pepper, chili powder, oregano, garlic and hot pepper sauce. Cook, stirring, approximately 5 minutes. Add beans, stewed tomatoes and green chiles. Reduce heat and simmer 10 minutes. Stir in tomato soup and heat a few minutes more. Serve.

"Quick and easy chili for a cold winter day."

Anita Huckert   **Greenfield Junior High School, Bakersfield, CA**

San Antonio Beef Stew

Serves: 4   Prep time: 30 minutes

  1 boneless beef sirloin steak, cut $3/4$" thick (about 1 pound)
  1 tablespoon vegetable oil
  $1/4$ teaspoon salt
  1 (13.75 to 14.5 ounce) can ready-to-serve beef broth
  $3/4$ cup Pace Picante Sauce
  2 medium zucchini, cut lengthwise in half, sliced crosswise $3/4$" thick
  1 large red bell pepper, cut into 1" pieces
  1 $1/2$ teaspoons ground cumin
  2 tablespoons cornstarch
  $1/4$ cup water
  Garnish: sour cream, chopped fresh cilantro

Trim fat from steak. Cut lengthwise in half and then crosswise into
$1/2$" thick strips. In Dutch oven, heat oil over medium-high heat until
hot. Add beef ($1/2$ at a time) and stir-fry 2 minutes or until outside
surface is no longer pink. (Do not overcook.) Remove from pan;
season with salt. Set aside. In same pan, combine broth, picante
sauce, zucchini, bell pepper and cumin. Bring to a boil; reduce heat
to medium-low. Simmer 10 minutes or until vegetables are crisp-
tender. Add cornstarch mixture to stew; cook and stir 1 to 2 minutes
or until sauce is thickened and bubbly. Return beef to pan. Serve
with sour cream and cilantro, if desired.

National Cattleman's Beef Association   **Chicago, IL**

Skillet Chili-Mac

Serves: 6   Prep time: 10 minutes, Cook: 20 minutes

  1 pound lean ground beef
  1 medium onion, diced
  1 (15 ounce) can red chili beans, drained
  1 small can kidney beans, drained
  1 (8 ounce) can tomato sauce
  1 (14 ounce) can tomatoes, diced
  1 cup elbow macaroni
  1 (4 ounce) can diced green chiles
  2 teaspoons chili powder
  $1/4$ teaspoon garlic salt
  1 teaspoon cayenne pepper
  $1/2$ cup cheddar cheese, shredded
  $1/4$ cup Monterey Jack or mozzarella cheese, shredded
  $1/2$ cup water

In a large skillet, cook meat and onion until meat is browned; drain
fat. Stir in beans, tomato sauce, undrained tomatoes, uncooked pasta,
green chiles, chili powder, garlic salt, cayenne and $1/2$ cup water.
Bring to a boil; reduce heat, cover and simmer 20 minutes, stirring

often. Top with cheese, cover & heat 2 minutes, or until cheese melts.

Julie Gibbons   **Chemawa Middle School, Riverside, CA**

Skillet Hamburger Noodle Supper
Serves: 4 - 6   Prep time: 10 minutes, Cook: 20 minutes

- $1/_2$ pound hamburger or ground turkey
- $1/_2$ cup onion, chopped
- $1/_2$ cup green pepper, chopped
- $1/_2$ teaspoon basil
- $1/_2$ teaspoon oregano
- 3 cups Campbell's condensed tomato soup
- 3 cups water
- 2 cups macaroni noodles
- 2 teaspoons lemon juice

Brown meat, onion, peppers, basil and oregano in large skillet. Stir in soup, water, macaroni and lemon juice and heat to boiling. Reduce heat to low and cook approximately 20 minutes.

"This is better than a Hamburger Helper.
You can add frozen peas for variety and added nutrients."

Eilene Hickman   **Bonanza High School, Las Vegas, NV**

Sloppy Chili Cheese Sandwich
Serves: 4   Prep time: 10 minutes

- 2 buns, hot dog or hamburger, split in half
- 2 cups chili, with or without beans
- $1/_2$ cup nacho cheese sauce
- *Garnish:* salsa (optional)

Put split buns on cookie sheet and place under broiler. Toast to a golden brown, checking very carefully to avoid burning. Put chili in casserole dish with a lid and microwave 2 to 3 minutes on HIGH. Put nacho cheese sauce in a liquid measuring cup and cover with paper towel. Microwave 1 minute. Spoon warm chili over toasted buns, spoon nacho cheese sauce on top. Garnish with salsa, if desired.

Marianne Traw   **Ball Junior High School, Anaheim, CA**

Spanish Noodles
Serves: 4   Prep time: 20 minutes, Cook: 25 minutes

- 2 slices bacon
- $1/_2$ cup celery, chopped
- 1 pound ground beef
- 1 (28 ounce) can tomatoes, quartered
- $1/_2$ cup green pepper, chopped
- 1 teaspoon salt
- dash pepper
- 4 ounces noodles, uncooked

Cook bacon until crisp; drain, reserving drippings. Crumble bacon and set aside. Add celery to drippings in skillet and cook until tender. Add ground beef, brown slightly. Add tomatoes, green pepper, salt and pepper. Stir in uncooked noodles. Cover and cook over low heat for 25 minutes or until tender. Stir in bacon.

"Macaroni may be substituted for noodles. Leftover diced roast beef may be used in place of ground beef. A 4-H member's favorite."

Mary Lash   **Paramount High School, Paramount, CA**

Spicy Cheese Surprise Burgers
Serves: 4   Prep time: 15 minutes, Cook: 10 minutes

1 pound ground beef
4 slices cheddar cheese
2 green onions, sliced
$^1/_2$ cup picante sauce
1 (8 ounce) can tomato sauce

Shape ground beef into 8 (3 $^1/_2$") patties. Place 1 slice cheese and 1 teaspoonful onions in center of 4 of the patties. Top each with remaining patties; press edges to seal. In large skillet over medium-high heat, cook patties 2 to 3 minutes on each side or until browned; drain excess fat. Spoon picante sauce and tomato sauce over patties. Reduce heat to low; cover and simmer 10 minutes or until heated.

Joyce Grohmann   **Los Amigos High School, Fountain Valley, CA**

Super Spuds
Serves: 4   Prep time: 20 minutes, Microwave 10 minutes 10 minutes

4 large baking potatoes
Italian style:
1 (15.5 ounce) jar spaghetti sauce with meat
$^1/_2$ cup pepperoni, chopped
1 cup mozzarella cheese, shredded
Texas style:
1 (15.5 ounce) can chili with beans
1 $^1/_2$ cups cheddar cheese, shredded
1 green onion, sliced

Scrub baking potatoes with a vegetable brush to remove surface dirt. Poke holes in potatoes with fork. Microwave on HIGH 5 minutes; turn over and move them 2" or 3" in any direction. Microwave on HIGH another 5 minutes. Remove from microwave and wrap in foil. Let stand 5 to 10 minutes. Meanwhile, prepare desired topping.
Italian style: Heat spaghetti sauce and pepperoni together in saucepan. Spoon over cooked potatoes and sprinkle with shredded cheese. *Texas style:* Heat chili in saucepan with 1 cup shredded cheese. Spoon over cooked potatoes and sprinkle with remaining

cheese. Top with green onion. When ready to serve, remove potatoes from foil and roll gently in hands (using hot pads). Cut a criss cross in top, push ends up and spoon hot topper over potatoes.

Linda Stroup   **Virgin Valley High School, Mesquite, NV**

Sweet-Sour Meat Balls
Serves: 6   Prep time: 10 minutes, Microwave: 15 minutes

    1 pound ground beef
    1 onion, finely chopped (or minced onion flakes)
    $3/_4$ teaspoon seasoned salt
    1 (10.75 ounce) can tomato soup
    3 tablespoons lemon juice
    $1/_4$ cup brown sugar
    1 (13.25 ounce) can pineapple chunks, drained

Roll ground beef into small meat balls; set aside. In a 9" square glass cake pan, combine onion, seasoned salt, tomato soup, lemon juice and brown sugar. Cook in microwave on HIGH 7 minutes, stirring twice during cooking. Place meatballs in sauce, spooning some sauce over top. Microwave 7 minutes on HIGH, turning dish once during cooking. Add drained pineapple chunks and cook on HIGH 1 minute more. Serve with toothpicks.

"A fast appetizer that company and my family always enjoy."

Faye Nielsen   **Rosemead High School, Rosemead, CA**

Szechwan Beef
Serves: 4   Prep time: 20 minutes

    2 tablespoons soy sauce
    1 tablespoon dry sherry
    2 teaspoons sugar
    $1/_2$ teaspoon cornstarch
    1 pound lean boneless beef steak (top round, flank or sirloin)
    2 tablespoons salad oil
    10 dried hot red chiles
    2 large carrots, cut into 3" julienne strips
    1 (8 ounce) can bamboo shoots, sliced, drained
    Garnish: fresh cilantro (optional)

Stir together soy sauce, dry sherry, sugar and cornstarch; set aside. Cut beef with the grain into 1 $1/_2$" wide strips; then cut each strip across grain into $1/_8$" thick slanting strips; set aside. Place a wok over high heat; add oil. When oil is hot, add chiles and cook, stirring, until chiles just begin to char. Remove chiles from wok; set aside. Add beef to wok and stir-fry until browned, 1 $1/_2$ to 2 minutes. Remove from wok; set aside. Stir fry carrots about 3 minutes, add bamboo shoots and stir-fry 1 minute more. Return meat and chiles to wok. Stir cooking sauce and add to wok. Stir until sauce boils and thickens. Garnish with cilantro, if desired.

"Students love to do a stir-fry unit."

Ramona Anderson   **Mira Mesa High School, San Diego, CA**

Tamale Casserole

Serves: 6   Prep time: 5 minutes, Bake: 30 minutes

2 cans hot tamales
1 small bag Fritos corn chips
1 large onion, chopped
2 cans chili, with beans
8 ounces cheese, grated

Preheat oven to 400 degrees. Using square casserole dish, layer bottom with 1 can tamales, top with half of the corn chips, $1/2$ chopped onion and 1 can chili. Repeat layers and top with grated cheese. Bake 30 minutes.

"Warms you right up on a cold night!"

Debbie Rothe   **Alta Loma High School, Alta Loma, CA**

Tamale Pie In A Skillet

Serves: 6 - 8   Prep time: 15 minutes, Cook: 20 minutes

1 onion, chopped
1 pound ground beef
1 (16 ounce) can stewed tomatoes
1 (17 ounce) can corn, undrained
1 cup sour cream
1 (4.5 ounce) can olives, sliced
1 cup corn meal
2 teaspoons salt
1 tablespoon chili powder
$1/2$ teaspoon cumin (optional)
2 cups Monterey jack cheese, shredded

Using a 10" or 12" skillet with lid, brown beef with onion; drain excess grease. Add tomatoes, corn with liquid, sour cream, corn meal, olives and seasonings. Stir until thoroughly mixed. Cover and simmer 20 minutes. Sprinkle with shredded cheese and serve.

"This recipe came to me from Wallowa County Cowbelles in N.E Oregon. It is one of the best tamale pies I have tasted!"

Maria Fregulia   **Lassen High School, Susanville, CA**

Teriyaki Ribbon Steak Marinade
Serves: 8   Prep time: 30 minutes

Marinade:
$1/4$ cup water or oil
2 tablespoons sugar
$1/3$ cup burgundy wine
$1/2$ teaspoon ginger
$1/4$ cup onion, minced
garlic, to taste
4 to 5 pounds tri-tip steak

Blend marinade ingredients together to dissolve. Turn meat several times in marinade at least 30 minutes to one hour. Drain and cook as desired.

*"I don't know anyone who doesn't love this recipe.
In a pinch, you can substitute red wine vinegar for burgundy wine."*

Diane Lizardi   **Downey High School, Downey, CA**

Teriyaki Steak
Serves: 4   Prep time: 30 minutes

$1/2$ cup soy sauce
$1/4$ cup water
$1/4$ cup catsup
1 $1/2$ " fresh ginger root, peeled, grated (or 1 teaspoon dried)
1 tablespoon fresh rosemary (or 1 teaspoon dried)
2 cloves garlic, minced
1 pound sirloin steak
2 tablespoons oil, for cooking
2 cups Japanese sticky rice, cooked

Mix soy sauce, water, catsup, ginger, rosemary and garlic in a 9" x 13" container. Slice steak into 2" x $1/2$" strips; marinate in pan 20 minutes, stirring occasionally. Heat oil in skillet on high. Fry steak pieces to desired doneness, 5 to 10 minutes; remove meat from pan. Reduce heat to medium and add remaining marinade; heat. Serve steak on top of prepared sticky rice and pour marinade over meat.
NOTE: Soy sauce is salty - you may desire to have cooked marinade served on the side.

*"This has become our family's favorite meal
and is requested for all special occasions."*

Carole Call   **Costa Mesa High School, Costa Mesa, CA**

Tijuana Torte

Serves: 8   Prep time: 20 minutes, Bake: 20 minutes

1 pound ground beef
1 onion, chopped
1 (15 ounce) can stewed tomatoes
1 (8 ounce) can tomato sauce
1 (4 ounce) can diced green chiles
1 package taco seasoning mix
1 (14 ounce) can corn
6 to 8 flour tortillas
1 pound cheddar cheese, grated
Garnish: sour cream

Preheat oven to 350 degrees. Brown ground beef with onion in a skillet; drain excess fat. Add stewed tomatoes, tomato sauce, chiles, seasoning mix and corn; simmer 10 minutes. In a 9" x 13" baking dish, layer tortillas, meat mixture and cheese, lasagne style. Bake 20 minutes, or until cheese is bubbly. Top with sour cream.

"One of my students at La Habra High School, Lee Malchow, gave me this recipe. It met with rave reviews from students, staff, and parents who tried it at Open House. (Each lab group in class made a half recipe.)"

Beth Swift   **La Habra High School, La Habra, CA**

Top Ramen Dinner

Serves: 4 - 6   Prep time: 20 minutes

1 $1/2$ pounds ground beef
2 cups water
2 packages Top Ramen with seasoning packets
2 cups frozen mixed vegetables
$1/4$ teaspoon ground ginger
2 tablespoons green onion, chopped

Brown meat in large 10" skillet; remove from pan and set aside. Add water and both packages ramen noodles, 1 seasoning packet from noodles, frozen vegetables and ginger to skillet; bring to a boil. Reduce heat, cover, and simmer 3 minutes. Stir in second seasoning packet, browned meat and green onions; cook 3 minutes more. Serve immediately.

"My daughter introduced me to this recipe and now is it a favorite 'quickie' for any busy day!"

Sandra Robertson   **Whittier High School, Whittier, CA**

Easy Taco Pizza
20 min. of preparation.
Page 98

Ranchero Wrap-ups
10 min. of preparation.
Page 71

Island Shrimp Wrap
15 min. of preparation.
Page 108

Pork Entrées
Chops • Casserole • Stir Fry

Apricot Pork Chops
Serves: 6   Prep time: 10 minutes, Cook: 30 minutes

    6 pork chops
    1 (#303) can apricot halves
    1 (10.75 ounce) can cream of chicken soup
    $^1/_2$ cup sour cream
    2 tablespoons green onion, chopped (tops included)
    3 cups rice, cooked

In skillet, brown pork chops; pour off fat. While chops are browning, drain apricots, reserving $^1/_4$ cup syrup. Mix soup, sour cream, apricot syrup and green onions and add to pork chops. Cover and simmer 25 minutes or until chops are tender, stirring occasionally. Add apricots and cook 5 minutes more. Serve over cooked rice.

Ann Hardman   **Livermore High School, Livermore, CA**

Camping Breakfast aka "Garbage"
Serves: 4   Prep time: 30 minutes

    1 (12 ounce) tube breakfast sausage (hot or mild)
    1 medium onion, chopped
    1 bell pepper, chopped
    3 medium potatoes, baked, cooled, cut into cubes
    4 eggs, beaten

Break up sausage in skillet; add onion and bell pepper and cook over medium heat until sausage is done and vegetables are tender. Stir in potatoes, cook until lightly browned. Add eggs and stir until eggs are set and firm. Serve immediately. NOTE: We often add leftovers like grated cheese, cooked vegetables or chicken, etc.

"This is a favorite camping recipe of our family. It was named by our niece who said 'This stuff looks like garbage!' We serve it for breakfast every June, by the river, under the trees, in Yosemite!"

Carolyn McBride   **Arcadia High School, Arcadia, CA**

Caraway Sauerkraut with Knackwurst

Serves: 6   Prep time: 10 minutes, Cook: 20 minutes

2 (1 pound) cans sauerkraut
1 $^1/_2$ cups apple juice or cider
1 tablespoon caraway seeds
1 pound knackwurst sausage

Drain sauerkraut in colander, rinse well under cold water and drain
again. In 4 quart Dutch oven, combine sauerkraut, apple juice and
caraway seeds. Cover and bring to a boil. Wash sausage and dry.
Pierce with a fork and place on top of sauerkraut; reduce heat and
simmer gently, covered, 20 minutes, or until heated through.

*"Good and quick German recipe. I serve this with rye bread
and German style potato salad. Yum!"*

Joanne Montoy   **Esperanza High School, Anaheim, CA**

Company Casserole

Serves: 4- 6   Prep time: 15 minutes, Bake: 1 hour, 30 minutes

1 pound sausage
1 onion, chopped
1 cup rice, uncooked
2 packages dry chicken noodle soup mix
1 can cream of mushroom soup
1 rib celery, chopped
$^1/_2$ red or green bell pepper, chopped
4 $^1/_2$ cups water

Preheat oven to 350 degrees. Brown sausage; drain. Combine
remaining ingredients with sausage, mixing well. Pour into a 13" x 9"
baking dish. Cover with foil and bake 1 hour; remove foil, stir and
bake 30 minutes more.

"My students prepared this dish for the parent volunteer brunch each spring."

Diane Castro   **Temecula Valley High School, Temecula, CA**

Easy Taco Pizza

Serves: 6   Prep time: 20 minutes, Bake: 18 - 22 minutes

$^1/_2$ pound ground pork
$^1/_2$ packet (2 tablespoons) taco seasoning
1 package pizza crust mix OR 1 (12") homemade pizza crust
1 cup salsa
1 cup reduced fat Colby jack cheese, shredded
$^2/_3$ cup lowfat tortilla chips, coarsely crushed
1 $^1/_2$ cups lettuce, shredded
2 tablespoons ripe olives, sliced (optional)

Preheat oven to 400 degrees. Cook ground pork with taco seasoning
mix in large skillet over medium heat for approximately 5 minutes or

until pork is no longer pink. Prepare pizza crust according to package
directions. Spread crust evenly on greased 12" pizza pan and top
evenly with salsa. Sprinkle on taco meat, cheese and tortilla chips.
Bake 18 to 22 minutes or until crust is golden grown. Remove from
oven. Top with shredded lettuce and olives and serve.

National Pork Producers Council   **Des Moines, IA**

Ham and Asian Noodles
Serves: 4   Prep time: 20 minutes

    2 cups water
    1 (16 ounce) package broccoli, carrots and water chestnuts, frozen
    2 packages Oriental flavor instant ramen noodles, with seasoning packets
    1/4 teaspoon ground ginger
    1 ham steak
    2 tablespoons green onions, thinly sliced

In a large nonstick skillet, combine 2 cups water, frozen vegetables,
noodles (broken into pieces), ginger and seasoning packets; bring to
a boil. While coming to a boil, dice ham steak into bite-sized pieces.
Reduce heat; cover and simmer 3 minutes, or until noodles are done,
stirring occasionally. Add ham to skillet and heat. Stir in green
onions and serve.

*"Keep 2 packages of Ramen noodles in your pantry, and you can make this in a
pinch with beef and chicken leftovers too! I like it with leftover pork roast!"*

Angela Croce   **Mira Mesa High School, San Diego, CA**

Ham Struedel
Serves: 4   Prep time: 15 minutes, Bake: 15 - 17 minutes

    6 green onions, chopped
    1 1/2 cups rice, cooked
    1 cup Swiss cheese, shredded
    2 tablespoons paprika
    1 tablespoon caraway seeds
    2 tablespoons capers
    6 sheets filo dough
    1/3 cup butter, melted
    1/2 pound cooked ham, thinly sliced
    1/3 cup sour cream
    3 tablespoons Dijon mustard, coarse grain

Preheat oven to 400 degrees. Mix onions, rice, cheese, paprika,
caraway seeds and capers. Lay 1 filo sheet flat and brush lightly with
butter. Repeat with remaining 5 sheets filo dough. Lay ham slices
over filo, overlapping as needed. Evenly pat rice mixture over ham.
Roll filo into roll and place seam side down on a buttered baking
sheet. Lightly brush struedel with butter. Bake until golden brown all

over, 15 to 17 minutes. Mix sour cream and mustard together. Using 2 wide spatulas, slide struedel onto a platter, cut into thick slices and garnish with Dijon sauce and chopped chives.

"This struedel looks beautiful with a salad!"

Leilani Neiner   **Fontana High School, Fontana, CA**

Luau Pizza

Serves: 6   Prep time: 10 minutes, Bake: 13 minutes

1 (10 ounce) thin crust Italian bread shell
2 cups mozzarella cheese, shredded, divided
1 cup pineapple tidbits in juice, drained
4 slices Canadian bacon (about 2 ounces)
1 cup fresh mushrooms, sliced
$1/4$ cup green bell pepper, chopped
$1/4$ cup Parmesan cheese, grated

Preheat oven to 450 degrees. Place bread shell on baking stone or sheet. Sprinkle with 1 cup mozzarella cheese. Cover evenly with pineapple tidbits. Stack Canadian bacon slices and cut into eighths. Arrange over pineapple. Sprinkle mushrooms and bell peppers evenly and top with remaining mozzarella and Parmesan cheeses. Bake 13 to 17 minutes or until cheese is melted. Cut into wedges and serve.

"Great as snack or with green salad for dinner."

Robin Ali   **Nevada Union High School, Grass Valley, CA**

Oven Baked Pork Loin Chops

Serves: 2 - 4   Prep time: 15 minutes, Bake: 35 - 45 minutes

nonstick cooking spray
4 pork loin chops, $1/2$" to $3/4$" thick
1 medium onion, thinly sliced
1 can golden mushroom soup
$1/2$ to $2/3$ can evaporated nonfat milk
$1/2$ cup almonds, pecans or cashews, slivered

Preheat oven to 350 degrees. Spray a rectangle baking dish with nonstick cooking spray. Arrange pork loin chops in dish in single layer. Arrange sliced onion evenly over chops. Stir together mushroom soup and milk until well blended; pour over meat. Cover with foil and bake 30 minutes. Uncover and sprinkle with slivered nuts. Bake additional 5 to 10 minutes, or until meat is done. NOTE: This can be prepared earlier in the day. Seal and refrigerate, then pop it into the oven 1 hour before you want to eat.

"Serve over steamed rice or noodles with a side dish of steamed vegetables."

Judi Topp   **A.B. Miller High School, Fontana, CA**

Pasta Prosciutto Supper

Serves: 4   Prep time: 20 minutes

    8 ounces pasta
    1 tablespoon olive oil
    1 teaspoon garlic, crushed
    3 green onions, chopped
    $^3/_4$ cup chicken broth
    8 ounces asparagus
    4 ounces prosciutto, chopped
    $^1/_2$ cup Parmesan cheese, grated

Cook pasta accordingly to package. While pasta cooks, heat olive oil in pan and saute green onion with garlic for 2 minutes. Add chicken broth, asparagus and prosciutto; heat through. Add drained pasta to broth mixture. Toss with Parmesan cheese.

"This recipe was a late night invention from ingredients on hand. It turned out to be a winner!"

Jill Burnham   **Bloomington High School, Bloomington, CA**

Penne Pasta With Sausage

Serves: 4   Prep time: 30 minutes

    12 ounces penne pasta
    2 tablespoons olive oil
    $^1/_2$ pound Italian sausage
    $^1/_2$ onion, chopped
    1 teaspoon garlic, minced
    3 ounces red bell pepper, roasted, chopped
    1 (26 ounce) jar marinara sauce
    1 $^1/_2$ cups fresh spinach
    Garnish: Parmesan cheese, grated

Bring a large pot of water to boil; cook pasta 10 minutes. Meanwhile, saute olive oil with sausage, onion and garlic in large skillet for 6 minutes, stirring occasionally. Drain off excess fat. Stir in peppers and sauce and bring to a boil. Simmer about 4 minutes. Stir in spinach and cook 1 minute longer, until wilted and heated through. Drain pasta and pour onto serving platter. Pour sauce over pasta and sprinkle with grated Parmesan cheese.

"This recipe was given to me by our health teacher. It is excellent!"

Debbie Harvey   **Amador Valley High School, Pleasanton, CA**

Pork Tenderloin With Balsamic Cranberry Sauce

Serves: 2   Prep time: 30 minutes

   1 $\frac{1}{2}$ tablespoons butter, divided
   1 (8 to 10 ounce) pork tenderloin
   salt and pepper, to taste
   $\frac{1}{2}$ cup onion, chopped
   1 tablespoon fresh rosemary, chopped
   $\frac{1}{2}$ cup low-salt chicken broth
   $\frac{1}{3}$ cup whole berry cranberry sauce
   1 tablespoon balsamic vinegar

Preheat oven to 450 degrees. Melt $\frac{1}{2}$ tablespoon butter in heavy large ovenproof skillet over medium-high heat. Sprinkle pork with salt and pepper. Sear pork on all sides, about 2 minutes. Place skillet with pork in oven and roast until thermometer inserted in center registers 155 degrees, about 10 minutes. Meanwhile, melt remaining 1 tablespoon butter in heavy medium skillet over medium-high heat. Add onion and rosemary and saute until onion softens, about 3 minutes. Add broth, cranberry sauce and vinegar and whisk until cranberry sauce melts, about 2 minutes. Transfer pork to work surface. Scrape any juices from large skillet into cranberry mixture. Boil until sauce has reduced enough to coat spoon thickly, about 6 minutes. Season with salt and pepper. Slice pork and serve with sauce.

"An elegant entree for a special evening that is quick and easy."

Julie Shelburne   **Tulare Union High School, Tulare, CA**

San Francisco Pork Chops

Serves: 4   Prep time: 20 minutes, Cook: 10 minutes

   $\frac{3}{4}$ cup dry sherry or apple juice, or $\frac{3}{8}$ cups of each
   6 tablespoons dark brown sugar
   6 tablespoons soy sauce
   1 teaspoon red pepper flakes (adjust to your taste)
   1 teaspoon olive oil
   4 lean, boneless pork chops
   salt and pepper, to taste
   4 cups egg noodles
   2 tablespoons cornstarch
   $\frac{1}{4}$ cup water
   Garnish: red and green bell pepper

In a small bowl, combine sherry or juice, brown sugar, soy sauce and pepper flakes; set aside. In hot skillet, heat oil. Season chops with salt and pepper to taste; brown in oil. Pour sauce over chops, reduce heat, cover and simmer 10 minutes. Meanwhile, prepare noodles as directed on package. Drain noodles, transfer to platter. Place chops on top of noodles. Cover to keep warm. Stir together corn starch and water. Thicken the sauce remaining in skillet by gradually stirring in cornstarch mixture over low heat. Once thickened, pour sauce over chops and noodles. Garnish with bell peppers and serve.

"I got this recipe from a local radio show. It really is simple but tasty."

Debby Truitt   **Woodland High School, Woodland, CA**

Stir-Fried Pork & Vegetables

Serves: 2   Prep time: 25 minutes

- 1 tablespoon peanut oil
- $1/2$ pound pork butt, thinly sliced OR lean country sparerib
- $1/4$ cup green onion, sliced
- $1/2$ cup celery, thinly sliced
- 5 (medium) mushrooms, thinly sliced
- $1/2$ teaspoon dry chicken bouillon
- 3 tablespoons water, divided
- 1 teaspoon soy sauce
- $1/2$ to $3/4$ cup fresh spinach leaves
- $1/2$ cup bean sprouts
- 1 teaspoon cornstarch
- 1 cup rice, cooked
- *Garnish:* 1 small tomato, chopped, 2 tablespoons cashew pieces

Heat peanut oil on high heat in wok or skillet. Add sliced pork and stir-fry until pink color disappears. Add green onion, celery and mushrooms. In small custard cup, mix chicken bouillon with 2 tablespoons water; stir in soy sauce and pour over vegetables. Stir to toss; reduce heat to medium and cover pan. Cook 2 to 3 minutes. Mix together cornstarch and 1 tablespoon water. Add to skillet; stir to thicken. Serve cover hot cooked rice. Garnish with chopped tomatoes and cashew pieces.

"Stir frying is so quick. Start rice at first so it is ready when stir-fry is ready. Adapt this basic recipe to available meats and vegetables."

Carla Escola   **Ripon High School, Ripon, CA**

Torta Rustica

Serves: 12   Prep time: 30 minutes, Bake: 35 - 40 minutes

- 1 package Hot Yeast Roll mix
- $3/4$ pound Italian sausage, cooked, sliced
- $1/4$ cup parsley, finely chopped
- $1/4$ cup Parmesan cheese, grated
- $3/4$ cup canned, peeled tomatoes, well drained
- 1 cup mozzarella cheese, grated
- 1 egg, well beaten

Prepare hot yeast roll mix as directed on package. Divide dough in half; roll one portion on floured board into a 9" round. Fit dough in bottom of a greased 9" springform pan. Spread cooked sausages evenly over dough in pan. Top with layers of parsley, Parmesan cheese, canned tomato and mozzarella cheese. Roll remaining dough into 9" square. Cut in strips about 1" wide. Weave strips over filling in a lattice pattern, tucking ends of dough down around filling at pan rim. Brush surface of dough with beaten egg. Bake on lowest rack of oven 35 to 40 minutes.

"A great afternoon luncheon or picnic dish!"

Betty Wells   **Bidwell Junior High School, Chico, CA**

Well-Dressed Pork
Serves: 8   Prep time: 30 minutes

1 cup broccoli, chopped
2 cups carrots, sliced
2 tablespoons vegetable oil
1 $^1/_2$ pounds boneless pork chops, cut in $^3/_4$" cubes
2 cloves garlic, finely chopped
$^1/_3$ cup green onion, finely chopped
2 tablespoons butter
2 tablespoons flour
2 cups milk
$^1/_4$ + $^1/_3$ cup Parmesan cheese, grated, divided
12 ounces bow tie pasta, cooked
$^1/_3$ cup Parmesan cheese, grated
2 large tomatoes, diced
2 tablespoons fresh parsley, chopped
salt and ground black pepper, to taste

Place broccoli and carrots in medium saucepan; add about 1" of water. Cook over medium-high heat until tender. Drain; set aside. Heat oil in large skillet over medium-high heat until hot. Add pork and garlic; cook 5 to 10 minutes, or until pork is no longer pink. Add green onions and saute 1 minute. *White Sauce:* melt butter in small saucepan over medium heat. Blend flour and milk; add to saucepan. Cook, stirring constantly until mixture is smooth and thickened. Stir in $^1/_4$ cup Parmesan cheese. In large casserole dish, combine pasta, pork mixture, vegetables and white sauce. Top with remaining $^1/_3$ cup Parmesan cheese, tomatoes, parsley, salt and pepper. Toss and serve.

National Pork Producers Council   **Des Moines, IA**

Seafood

Shrimp • Fish • Chowder

Baked Cod Parmesan

Serves: 4   Prep time: 5 minutes, Bake: 8 - 10 minutes

    2 tablespoons flour
    3 tablespoons cornmeal
    $1/4$ teaspoon onion salt
    $1/8$ teaspoon pepper
    3 tablespoons butter or margarine
    1 pound cod fillets, thawed
    $1/4$ cup Parmesan cheese, grated

Preheat oven to 450 degrees. Combine flour, cornmeal and seasonings. In shallow baking dish, melt butter or margarine. Dredge cod in flour mixture; place in dish. Turn cod to coat with butter; sprinkle with Parmesan cheese and bake 8 to 10 minutes.

Sharon Both   **Azusa High School, Azusa, CA**

Broiled Seabass

Serves: 4   Prep time: 5 minutes, Cook: 10 - 12 minutes

    2 large seabass fillets
    1 container Contadina Pesto Sauce

Spread surface of fish generously with pesto sauce. Broil until edges of fish are slightly browned, about 10 to 12 minutes. Serve immediately.

Edna O'Neal   **Durango High School, Las Vegas , NV**

Easy Paella

Serves: 5   Prep time: 20 minutes

    1 (4 to 6 ounce) package rice pilaf mix OR 3 cups Texmati rice, prepared
    2 to 3 tablespoons butter
    1 teaspoon cajun seasoning
    1 teaspoon garlic, finely chopped
    8 ounces boneless, skinless chicken breast halves
    1 medium onion, cut into eighths
    1 (9 ounce) package frozen peas
    $1/2$ pound medium shrimp, cooked

Cook rice according to package directions. Meanwhile, in a 12" skillet, melt butter until sizzling. Stir in cajun seasoning and garlic. Add chicken and onion; cook over medium-high heat, stirring occasionally, until chicken is no longer pink, about 7 to 9 minutes. Stir in peas, shrimp and cooked rice. Continue cooking and stirring until peas and shrimp are heated through.

"This is a great recipe when in a hurry - I like to use the Texmati rice blend instead of the rice pilaf."

Cindy Johnson   **Orland High School, Orland, CA**

Fancy Salmon Fillets
Serves: 2   Prep time: 5 minutes, Cook: 10 - 12 minutes

2 medium-sized salmon fillets
1 teaspoon garlic, minced
1 teaspoon ginger, minced
3 tablespoons soy sauce
2 tablespoons honey
2 tablespoons lime juice
1 green onion, chopped

Combine all ingredients in a glass bowl. Cover and marinate in refrigerator for 20 minutes. Place on greased shallow pan and broil 10 to 12 minutes.

Edna O'Neal   **Durango High School, Las Vegas, NV**

Fish 'n Chips
Serves: 4   Prep time: 10 minutes, Bake: 12 - 15 minutes

1 cup potato chips, crushed
$1/4$ cup Parmesan cheese, grated
$1/4$ teaspoon thyme
1 pound fish fillets
$1/4$ cup milk
$1/4$ cup margarine, melted

Preheat oven to 500 degrees. Mix together crushed potato chips, Parmesan cheese and thyme in a shallow dish. Dip fish fillets in milk, then into coating mixture. Place in a greased baking dish and sprinkle with leftover coating mixture in places where it didn't stick. Drizzle fillets with melted margarine. Bake 12 to 15 minutes.

"You can make this healthier by using fat free potato chips and less margarine. It's still delicious!"

Penny Niadna   **Golden West High School, Visalia, CA**

Garlic Shrimp

Serves: 4   Prep time: 15 minutes

$1/_4$ cup olive oil
4 to 6 cloves garlic, minced
1 teaspoon red pepper flakes
1 bag frozen shrimp, peeled, deveined, thawed
2 tablespoons dry sherry
1 teaspoon paprika
2 tablespoons fresh lemon juice
salt and freshly ground pepper, to taste
Garnish: fresh chopped Italian parsley, lemon wedges

In a saute pan over medium heat, warm olive oil. Add garlic and red
pepper flakes and saute 1 minute. Raise heat to high and add shrimp,
sherry and paprika. Stir well, then saute, stirring briskly, until shrimp
turn opaque, about 3 minutes. Add lemon juice and season to taste
with salt and pepper. Sprinkle with parsley and serve hot, with lemon
wedges. NOTE: Lemon juice and sherry added during last minute of
cooking prevent shrimp from becoming tough. For more garlic flavor,
you may use the garlic and oil from marinated garlic sold in a jar.

"Have plenty of bread on hand to sop up the delicious pan juices!"

Liz Coleman   **Oroville High School, Oroville, CA**

Hallbut With Cheese Sauce

Serves: 4 - 6   Prep time: 10 minutes, Bake: 20 - 25 minutes

1 cup evaporated milk
$1/_4$ cup butter
3 to 4 tablespoons flour
1 teaspoon salt
1 $1/_2$ cups cheddar cheese, grated
dash cayenne pepper
1 $1/_4$ to 1 $1/_2$ teaspoons dry mustard
4 to 6 halibut fillets

Preheat oven to 350 degrees. Mix together milk, butter, flour and salt.
Stir in grated cheese (if too thick, can be thinned with water, broth
or white wine), cayenne and dry mustard. Place halibut fillets in a
buttered baking dish. Pour cheese sauce over top and bake,
uncovered, for 20 to 25 minutes.

"This is really good served on a bed of steamed rice, but can be served on egg
noodles and placed back into the hot oven for another 5 minutes, or until bubbly."

Eilene Hickman   **Bonanza High School, Las Vegas, NV**

Island Shrimp Wrap

Makes: 8 to 10 wraps   **Prep time: 15 minutes, Cook: 10 minutes**

>   8 to 10 skewers
>   40 medium shrimp, peeled, deveined
>   1 green bell pepper, cut into 2" pieces
>   1 red onion, sliced into 1" wide slices
>   1 (20 ounce) can pineapple chunks, drained
>   3/4 cup Lawry's Caribbean Jerk Marinade with Papaya Juice
>   8 - 10 (6") flour tortillas

Skewer 4 or 5 shrimp with alternating bell pepper, onion and pineapple chunks. Brush filled skewers liberally with Caribbean Jerk Marinade; grill or broil until shrimp are cooked and vegetables are crisp yet tender. Baste often. Place one skewer on each tortilla, pull skewer out and wrap up grilled food in tortilla. Serve warm or chilled.

"Wrap Party Tip: wrap fillings can be made up ahead and refrigerated. When ready to serve, place on buffet and let guests make their own wraps."

Lawry's Foods, Inc.   **Monrovia, CA**

Linguine With Clam Sauce

Serves: 4   **Prep time: 20 minutes**

>   1 (12 ounce) package linguine
>   3 cloves garlic, finely chopped
>   2 tablespoons olive oil
>   1/2 cube butter
>   1/4 cup lowfat or nonfat milk
>   1/4 cup dry white wine
>   2 cans clams, minced (do not drain)
>   1/4 cup fresh parsley, minced
>   1/2 cup Parmesan cheese, freshly grated
>   salt and pepper, to taste

Cook linguine as directed on package until al dente; drain and set aside. Saute garlic in olive oil and butter. Add milk, wine and clams. Toss with cooked, drained noodles. Stir in parsley and cheese. Season with salt and pepper.

"A modification of Don Cueno's (Black Bart Inn) since I cannot use cream."

Simone Clements   **Bret Harte Union High School, Altaville, CA**

Oven Fried Snapper

Serves: 6   **Prep time: 15 minutes, Bake: 12 - 15 minutes**

>   2 pounds red snapper
>   1/2 cup light olive oil
>   1 teaspoon salt
>   2 to 3 cloves garlic, pressed
>   1 cup Parmesan cheese, grated
>   1 cup dry bread crumbs

Rinse fish in cold water; pat dry with paper towels. Cut fish into 6 equal size serving portions. Combine oil, salt and garlic in oblong baking dish. Preheat oven to 500 degrees. Place fish in mixture. Let marinate 5 minutes; turn and marinate 5 minutes more. Remove fish from marinade. Mix Parmesan cheese and bread crumbs together. Coat fish with mixture and place on well greased cookie sheet. Bake 12 to 15 minutes.

Cheri Schuette   **Valley View Middle School, Simi Valley, CA**

Pesto Shrimp 'n Shells
Serves: 4   **Prep time: 20 minutes**

    1 tablespoon oil
    $^1/_2$ cup sun-dried tomatoes in oil, sliced
    1 pound shrimp, shelled, deveined
    1 package fresh pesto with basil sauce
    1 (medium) can olives, sliced
    $^1/_4$ cup pine nuts, toasted
    1 (16 ounce) package small or medium pasta shells, cooked
    Parmesan cheese, grated, to taste

In large skillet, heat oil over medium heat; saute sun-dried tomatoes with shrimp until shrimp turn pink. Stir in pesto sauce, olives, toasted pine nuts and cooked pasta; heat through, about 3 to 5 minutes. Stir again and top with Parmesan cheese, to taste.

*"I modified this recipe from a firefighter.
It validates their reputation as being great cooks!"*

Rebecca Harshbarger   **Temecula Valley High School, Temecula, CA**

Poached Salmon
Serves: 4 - 6   **Prep time: 10 minutes, Cook: 4 - 6 minutes**

    2 to 3 cups chicken broth
    4 ounces white wine (optional)
    1 to 2 teaspoons lemon zest
    2 tablespoons fresh dill or 2 teaspoons dried dill
    4 to 6 peppercorns
    4 to 6 ($^3/_4$ ounce) salmon fillets

In a large skillet, bring broth and wine to a boil. Add seasonings and simmer 2 minutes. Add salmon fillets and cover. Poach 4 to 6 minutes until fish flakes with a fork and has lost it's transparent color.

*"Serve with a vegetable and salad for a delightful, low-calorie meal.
This is an especially good meal for a warm evening
and any leftovers are great for lunch the next day!"*

Kathleen Fresquez   **Mountain View High School, El Monte, CA**

Salmon Patties

Serves: 5   Prep time: 20 minutes

    2 (15 ounce) cans salmon
    1 (sleeve) soda crackers, finely crushed
    2 eggs, beaten
    1 lemon, cut into wedges

Mix canned salmon, crackers and eggs in a bowl. Shape into patties similar to hamburger patties. Pan fry, turning once. Serve with lemon wedges.

"Creamed corn is a good side dish. I use 3 fry pans at the same time to speed up frying time."

Cheryl Moyle   **Olympus High School, Salt Lake City, UT**

Salmon With Lemon Pepper Seasoning

Serves: 4   Prep time: 5 minutes, Microwave: 8 minutes

    4 salmon fillets
    4 teaspoons butter
    2 teaspoons lemon pepper seasoning

Place salmon in an 8" x 8" glass pan. Dot with butter. Sprinkle lemon pepper seasoning over all. Cover with plastic wrap and cook in microwave 8 minutes on 80% power, rotating once during cooking.

"This is quick and easy to make, yet so wonderful that I often serve it to company."

Pat Hufnagel   **Esperanza High School, Anaheim, CA**

Salmon-Apple Pasta

Serves: 3   Prep time: 30 minutes

    8 ounces linguine
    2 tablespoons margarine, divided
    12 ounces salmon steaks, cut into $3/4$" chunks
    1 cup mushrooms, sliced
    1 cup asparagus spears, diagonally sliced
    $1/4$ cup onion, chopped
    $1/8$ teaspoon salt
    $1/8$ teaspoon pepper
    $1/4$ teaspoon oregano
    4 ounces half & half
    1 golden delicious apple, cored, cut into $1/2$" cubes
    Garnish: freshly grated Parmesan cheese

Cook linguine according to package directions; drain and set aside. Melt 1 tablespoon margarine in large frying pan; saute salmon chunks 5 minutes. Remove from pan and keep warm. Add remaining 1 tablespoon margarine to pan and saute mushrooms, asparagus and onion 2 minutes. Add salt, pepper, oregano and half & half; cook on high heat 1 minute more. Add apple, cooked salmon chunks and cook 30 seconds. Serve over hot linguine with freshly grated Parmesan cheese.

"A new way to enjoy salmon and vegetables in one dish. Use your favorite pasta."

Margo Olsen   **Amador Valley High School, Pleasanton, CA**

Sizzling Salmon Fajitas

Serves: 3   Prep time: 25 minutes

1 1/4 pounds salmon, boned, skinned, cut into 1" cubes
1 onion, thinly sliced
2 tablespoons lemon juice
1 teaspoon ground cumin
1 teaspoon fresh ginger, minced
1 1/2 teaspoons hot sauce
1/8 teaspoon crushed red pepper flakes
4 large leaves romaine lettuce
3 tomatoes, chopped
6 flour tortillas, warmed
Garnish: sour cream

In a large bowl, combine salmon, onion, lemon juice, cumin, ginger, hot sauce and chili flakes; mix well. Cover and chill 10 minutes. Meanwhile, shred lettuce, chop tomatoes; cover and chill separately until serving time. When ready to serve, heat a large nonstick frying pan over medium-high heat. When hot, add salmon mixture. Cook, stirring often, until fish is opaque, about 6 minutes. Serve immediately in warmed tortillas and top with lettuce and tomatoes. Garnish with sour cream.

"A great alternative when serving fish."

Teresa Hayes   **Buena High School, Ventura, CA**

Snappy Halibut Skillet

Serves: 4 - 6   Prep time: 7 minutes, Cook: 4 - 6 minutes

1 medium onion, sliced
1 clove garlic, crushed
1 tablespoon olive oil
1 (14.5 ounce) can Del Monte Diced Tomatoes with Green Pepper & Onion
1/4 cup salsa
1 1/2 pounds firm fish, such as halibut, red snapper or seabass

Cook onion and garlic in oil in skillet over medium-high heat until tender. Stir in tomatoes and salsa; cook 3 minutes. Add fish, cook 4 to 6 minutes or until fish flakes easily with fork. Serve with lime wedges, if desired. *Microwave Directions:* Combine onion, garlic and oil in 1 1/2 quart microwave dish. Cover and cook on HIGH 3 minutes. Stir in tomatoes and salsa. Top with fish. Cover and cook HIGH 3 to 4 minutes or until fish flakes easily with fork. Serve with lime wedges, if desired.

Del Monte Foods **San Francisco, CA**

Tortilla Tuna Bake
Serves: 4 **Prep time: 10 minutes, Bake: 45 - 50 minutes**

1 (6 $^1/_3$) ounce can tuna, drained
10 ounces broccoli, cooked
8 ounces cheddar cheese, shredded (divided)
1 (8 ounce) can Durkee French Fried Onions (divided)
1 (10.75) ounce can cream of mushroom soup
$^1/_2$ cup milk
6 (large) flour tortillas

Preheat oven to 350 degrees. Mix tuna, broccoli, 5 ounces cheese and half can of onions. In separate bowl, mix soup and milk. Pour $^3/_4$ of soup/milk mixture into tuna mixture. Spoon into flour tortillas and roll. Place tortillas in greased 9" x 13" baking dish. Pour remaining soup/milk mixture on top of tortillas. Bake, covered, 40 minutes. Put remaining cheese and onions on top and bake, uncovered, 5 to 10 minutes longer until cheese melts.

Eloise Hatfield **Poston Junior High School, Mesa, AZ**

Tuna Casserole In A Hurry
Serves: 2 - 3 **Prep time: 20 minutes**

1 (5 ounce) box favorite noodle mix, prepared with nonfat milk
    and low calorie margarine
1 rib celery, chopped
$^1/_2$ cup onion, chopped
1 can albacore tuna, drained

Prepare pasta according to package direction, adding chopped celery and onion. Flake tuna and stir into noodles. Serve immediately.

"Serves 1 hearty appetite or more depending on tuna craving."

Janet Riegel **Charter Oak High School, Covina, CA**

Tuna Delight

Serves: 6   Prep time: 15 minutes, Bake: 20 minutes

- 1 package wide egg noodles
- 2 tablespoons butter or margarine
- $1/2$ onion, diced
- $1/4$ cup all-purpose flour
- 1 teaspoon salt
- 1 teaspoon pepper
- 1 teaspoon garlic powder
- $1/2$ teaspoon dry mustard
- 1 cup milk
- 1 (10.75 ounce) can cream of mushroom soup
- 1 (12.5 ounce) can tuna, drained
- 1 bag frozen petite peas
- 1 cup cheddar cheese, shredded
- 2 cups potato chips, crushed

Prepare noodles according to package directions; drain and set aside. Preheat oven to 350 degrees. While noodles are cooking, melt butter in 3 quart saucepan over medium-high heat. Saute onion 2 to 3 minutes. Stir in flour, salt, pepper, garlic powder and dry mustard. Cook, stirring constantly until bubbly; remove from heat. Stir in milk and mushroom soup. Return to heat and bring to a boil, stirring constantly. Boil 1 minute. Stir in tuna, peas, cheddar cheese and cooked noodles. Pour into ungreased 2 quart casserole dish. Top with crushed potato chips and bake 20 minutes.

"A family favorite."

Donna Baker   **Redlands East Valley High School, Redlands, CA**

Meatless Entrées
Pasta • Pizza • Veggies

Baked Mostaccioli

Serves: 4 - 6   Prep time: 20 minutes, Bake: 20 minutes

     10 ounces mostaccioli
     20 ounces spaghetti sauce
     8 ounces ricotta cheese
     8 ounces mozzarella cheese, grated

Preheat oven to 350 degrees. Cook pasta according to package directions; drain. Combine sauce and ricotta cheese in a saucepan; add cooked pasta and stir well. Pour into a casserole dish. Sprinkle with grated mozzarella and bake 20 minutes.

"Very quick, easy and nutritious."

Bonnie Culp   **Montclair High School, Montclair, CA**

Best Ever Fettuccini

Serves: 4 - 6   Prep time: 30 minutes

     12 ounces fettuccini noodles (use $1/2$ spinach if desired)
     $1/2$ to 1 pound Polish sausage or bacon, sliced
     8 ounces mushrooms, fresh or canned, sliced
     4 to 5 egg yolks, beaten
     1 cup sour cream
     $1/2$ to 1 cup Parmesan cheese, grated
     salt and pepper, to taste

Cook fettuccini noodles as directed; drain and set aside. Fry Polish sausage or bacon; add mushrooms and saute lightly. Add cooked noodles. Stir in beaten egg yolks, sour cream, Parmesan cheese and salt and pepper to taste. Toss; put back over low heat to finish coating noodles.

"Use shrimp, scallops, slivered almonds, cashews, pork sausage...it's to die for!"

Sheri Rader   **Chaparral High School, Las Vegas, NV**

Bow Tie Pasta in Tomato Brie Sauce

Serves: 4 - 6   Prep time: 30 minutes

    1 (12 ounce) package bow tie pasta
    2 (14.5 ounce) cans Italian style diced tomatoes
    4 to 5 ounces brie, cubed (rind removed)
    fresh basil, chopped (optional)

Cook pasta according to package directions. While pasta cooks, heat tomatoes in a 4 quart saute pan or pot until it begins to boil. Add brie. Lower heat to simmer to melt brie. Drain pasta and fold into tomato sauce mixture. Serve immediately topped with chopped fresh basil.

"An impressive pasta dish for brie lovers, ready in less than 30 minutes!"

Angela Croce   **Mira Mesa High School, San Diego, CA**

Broccoli, Rice & Cheese Casserole

Serves: 6 -8   Prep time: 15 minutes, Microwave: 10 - 15 minutes

    1 cup water
    1 cup instant rice
    1 tablespoon margarine
    1 small onion, chopped
    1 can cream of mushroom soup
    1 (8 ounce) jar Cheez Whiz
    8 to 10 ounces broccoli, chopped

Bring water to a boil; add rice, cover and remove from heat. In skillet, melt margarine; saute onion. Add soup and Cheez Whiz, stirring to melt cheese. Stir in broccoli and rice. Place in microwave baking dish and microwave on HIGH 10 to 15 minutes.
NOTE: Can also be baked at 350 degrees 20 to 30 minutes.

"This is a family favorite."

Monica Carlson   **La Contenta Junior High School, Yucca Valley, CA**

Chili Pronto

Serves: 6   Prep time: 30 minutes

    $1/2$ cup onion, chopped
    2 cloves garlic, minced
    1 tablespoon oil
    2 tablespoons chili powder
    1 teaspoon ground cumin
    $1/2$ teaspoon oregano
    $1/2$ teaspoon red pepper flakes
    2 tablespoons tomato paste
    1 (16 ounce) can crushed tomatoes
    2 cups vegetable broth
    2 (29 ounce) cans pinto or red kidney beans
    salt and pepper, to taste

In a large saucepan, briefly cook onion and garlic in oil. Stir in spices, tomato paste, crushed tomatoes and vegetable broth. Bring to a boil; stir and reduce heat to simmer. Drain the liquid from the beans and add to saucepan. Allow chili to thicken before serving. Add salt and pepper, to taste.

"My family likes this chili served with a sprinkling of cheddar cheese on top. Served with cornbread and salad it makes a wonderful meal."

Linda Falkenstien   **Morro Bay High School, Morro Bay, CA**

Chili Spaghetti

Serves: 4   **Prep time: 15 minutes, Bake: 10 - 15 minutes**

    12 ounces spaghetti or desired pasta
    1 (15 ounce) can chili with beans
    1 cup cheddar/jack cheese combination, shredded

Cook pasta according to package directions. Meanwhile, heat chili in saucepan over medium heat. Drain cooked pasta and place in baking dish; top with heated chili and cover with shredded cheese. Bake 10 to 15 minutes at 325 degrees or cook in microwave on HIGH 3 to 5 minutes, until cheese is melted.

"Serve with mixed greens. Everyone in my family enjoys this meal. Always keep the chili in stock to take care of 'those' days!"

Judith Mahon   **Orangeview Junior High School, Anaheim, CA**

Corn and Chile Casserole

Serves: 4 - 6   **Prep time: 10 minutes, Bake: 20 minutes**

    $1/4$ cup margarine
    4 cups corn (1 $1/2$ pounds frozen)
    $1/2$ cup onion, finely chopped
    1 clove garlic, minced
    3 (small) cans green chiles, diced
    $1/2$ pound jack cheese, shredded

Preheat oven to 350 degrees. Melt margarine in saucepan. Add corn, onion, garlic and chiles. Cover and cook 5 minutes. Pour mixture into casserole dish and stir in cheese. Cover with lid and bake 20 minutes.

Cheri Schuette   **Valley View Middle School, Simi Valley, CA**

Delightful Veggie Quesadillas
Serves: 4 - 6   Prep time: 20 - 30 minutes

1 tablespoon margarine
1 cup green onion, chopped
1 cup fresh corn kernels (2 ears)
1 cup zucchini, unpeeled, diced
1 clove garlic, minced
1 large tomato, chopped
1 $1/2$ teaspoons jalapeño, seeded, minced
2 tablespoons fresh lemon juice
2 tablespoons fresh cilantro, minced
8 (8") flour tortillas
1 cup mozzarella, jack or cheddar cheese (or combination), shredded
Garnish: salsa

Heat margarine in skillet over medium heat. Add onion, corn, zucchini and garlic; saute 30 seconds. Add tomato and jalapeño; saute 4 minutes. Stir in lemon juice and cilantro; saute 3 minutes. Turn heat down to low to keep warm. Place 1 tortilla in a nonstick skillet over medium heat; top with $1/4$ cup cheese. Spoon $1/2$ cup filling over cheese; top with another tortilla. Cook 3 minutes, pressing down with a spatula until cheese melts. Turn carefully; cook until thoroughly heated, about 1 minute. Repeat with remaining tortillas. Cut each into quarters and serve with salsa.

"Flavorful, delicious, colorful...Yum!"

Dale Sheehan   **Santana High School, Santee, CA**

Fiesta Eggs
Serves: 6   Prep time: 20 minutes, Microwave: 6 $1/2$ minutes

4 frozen shredded potato patties
1 (11 ounce) can Campbell's nacho cheese soup, divided
8 eggs, slightly beaten
2 tablespoons milk
1 cup Monterey jack cheese, shredded
Garnish: sliced green onions, chopped red pepper

Prepare potato patties according to package directions. Meanwhile, in 3 quart microwave-safe bowl, stir $1/2$ can soup until smooth. Gradually blend in eggs. Cover with lid; microwave on HIGH 6 $1/2$ minutes or until eggs are nearly set, stirring 3 times during cooking. Let stand, covered, 2 minutes. *Sauce:* in 1 quart casserole, stir together remaining soup and milk until smooth. Cover with lid and microwave on HIGH 2 minutes or until hot, stirring once during cooking. Sprinkle $1/4$ cup cheese over each cooked potato patty. Arrange eggs on top and spoon about 2 tablespoons sauce over each. Garnish as desired. NOTE: For a Mexican flair, omit the potatoes and wrap eggs in warmed corn tortillas.

*"One of my students submitted this recipe for us to try as a class.
We did and it was a great success. Tasty, quick and easy!"*

Beth Kolberg-Bentle   **Rancho High School, N. Las Vegas, NV**

Funky Bean Casserole

Serves: 4   Prep time: 20 minutes

    1 pound ground beef
    1 small green pepper, chopped
    1 (14.5 ounce) jar salsa, chunky style
    1 (16 ounce) can black beans, undrained
    $^1/_2$ cup golden raisins

Cook beef with bell pepper in 12" nonstick skillet over medium heat 8
to 10 minutes, stirring occasionally, until beef is browned; drain
excess fat. Stir in remaining ingredients; reduce heat to low. Cover
and simmer 5 to 7 minutes, stirring occasionally, until hot.

"This is great served over rice. Great sweet and tangy combination."

Susan Eckert   **Basic High School, Henderson, NV**

Gardenburger Tacos

Serves: 2 - 4   Prep time: 20 minutes

    4 Gardenburger patties
    8 corn or flour tortillas
    $^1/_2$ head lettuce, shredded
    2 small tomatoes, diced
    1 cup cheese, shredded
    Garnish: taco sauce, guacamole

Microwave Gardenburgers according to package directions.
Meanwhile, heat tortillas in 350 degree oven for 5 to 10 minutes, until
warmed. Break up Gardenburger patties and place $^1/_2$ crumbled patty
in each tortilla. Top with lettuce, tomatoes and cheese. Garnish with
taco sauce and guacamole.

*"This is a quick, easy and lowfat meal. If you don't like Gardenburgers,
use more condiments."*

Karen Peters   **Vaca Peña Middle School, Vacaville, CA**

Green Spaghetti

Serves: 4   Prep time: 30 minutes

    1 pound spaghetti, cooked, drained
    10 ounces frozen spinach, chopped
    $^1/_4$ cup chicken or vegetable broth
    $^1/_2$ cup Parmesan cheese, grated
    $^1/_2$ cup milk or plain yogurt
    4 tablespoons butter (optional)

118

Prepare spaghetti according to package directions. Meanwhile, heat spinach in microwave until hot. Heat broth over low heat. Place spinach and it's liquid into blender. Add warmed broth and liquefy. Stir cheese and milk into spinach mixture. When spaghetti is done, drain and place in large bowl. Toss with butter, then spinach mixture.

"This is a great way to encourage kids to eat spinach.
My children love it and request it for special meals."

Mary M. Rector   **Valley High School, Las Vegas, NV**

Instant Enchiladas
Makes: 10   **Prep time: 10 minutes, Microwave: 10 minutes**
1 package Lawry's Enchilada Sauce Mix, prepared
1 (family pack) beef and bean burritos (Las Campanas, for example)
1 cup cheddar cheese, shredded
1 (small) can black olives, sliced, drained

Prepare enchilada sauce according to package directions. Place a small amount of sauce in bottom of microwave casserole dish. Place burritos over sauce and cover with remaining sauce. Top with shredded cheese and sliced olives. Microwave on HIGH 10 minutes.

"Prepackaged burritos come in different combinations.
Select any type depending on your taste."

Diana Geiger   **Tulare Western High School, Tulare, CA**

Italian Quesadillas
Serves: 4   **Prep time: 25 minutes**
$1/2$ cup fresh basil, shredded
1 cup marinara sauce
nonstick cooking spray
8 flour tortillas
1 cup cheddar cheese, grated
1 cup Monterey jack cheese, grated
4 tablespoons Parmesan cheese, grated
1 green bell pepper, thinly sliced
1 red bell pepper, thinly sliced
1 (4 ounce) can black olives, sliced
Garnish: sour cream, warm marinara sauce, bell pepper slices

Stir fresh chopped basil into marinara sauce and heat in saucepan over low heat. Heat a skillet on medium heat; spray with nonstick cooking spray.Place 1 tortilla in skillet and top with 2 tablespoons marinara sauce, $1/4$ cup cheddar, 1 tablespoon Parmesan, few slices bell peppers and few sliced olives. Sprinkle with $1/4$ cup jack cheese. Place second tortilla on top of stack. Cover skillet with lid and cook until cheeses are melted. Slide out onto a cutting board and assemble second, third and fourth as described above. Allow each quesadilla to cool 2 to 3 minutes before cutting, to firm up cheese. Cut into wedges. Serve with garnishes, as desired.

"When I'm in a big hurry, I use 2 skillets to speed up the cooking times. I serve this with fresh grapes, cantaloupe and a tossed green salad on busy midweek nights."

Priscilla Burns   **Pleasant Valley High School, Chico, CA**

Light Veggie Pasta Toss
Serves: 4   Prep time: 20 minutes

    8 cups fresh spinach, coarsely chopped
    8 cups hot, cooked cavatappi (6 ounces uncooked pasta)
    1 cup feta cheese, crumbled
    $1/4$ cup olive oil
    1 tablespoons fresh lemon juice
    $1/2$ teaspoon salt
    $1/2$ teaspoon pepper
    2 (19 ounce) cans garbanzo beans, drained
    4 cloves garlic, minced

Combine all ingredients in large salad bowl; toss and serve.

"This is a recipe from 'Cooking Light' magazine that we had on several warm summer nights - very refreshing. I use only 1 can of garbanzos and more feta for a main dish."

Donna Swennes   **El Capitan High School, Lakeside, CA**

Linguine and Vegetable Supreme
Serves: 4   Prep time: 30 minutes

    8 ounces linguine
    2 tablespoons butter or olive oil
    1 medium zucchini, grated
    1 medium carrot, grated
    $1/2$ onion, chopped
    4 ounces mozzarella cheese, grated
    $1/2$ cup milk
    $1/2$ teaspoon salt
    1 to 2 cloves garlic, chopped
    $1/4$ teaspoon dried basil leaves

Cook pasta according to package directions; drain. Heat oil or butter in large skillet over medium heat; saute zucchini, carrot and onion about 3 minutes. Add cooked linguine, cheese, milk, salt, garlic and basil. Turn heat off and mix together until cheese is melted. Serve immediately.

"Substitute any vegetables you want in this recipe. My students love this one!"

Debbie Powers   **Griffiths Middle School, Downey, CA**

120

Linguine With Vegetables

Serves: 4   Prep time: 30 minutes

- $^1/_2$ pound linguine or flat spaghetti
- 2 tablespoons butter or oil
- 1 clove garlic, minced
- 2 green onions, chopped
- 2 small zucchini, ends trimmed, thinly sliced
- $^1/_4$ pound mushrooms, sliced
- 1 medium tomato, peeled, chopped
- $^1/_2$ teaspoon dried basil
- $^1/_2$ teaspoon salt
- $^1/_4$ teaspoon pepper
- 1 cup provolone cheese, grated
- 3 tablespoons Parmesan cheese, grated
- 2 tablespoons parsley, chopped

In large saucepan, bring a large amount of salted water to a boil. Add pasta and cook over medium-high heat until pasta is tender; drain. Return pasta to saucepan. Heat butter or oil in large skillet or wok. Stir-fry garlic, green onion and zucchini 2 minutes. Add mushrooms and cook 1 minute. Add tomatoes, basil and seasonings and reduce heat. Simmer 3 to 4 minutes or until tender-crisp. Add vegetables to pasta, then add cheese and mix until cheese is melted. Sprinkle with parsley. Serve hot.

Roberta Marshall   Solano Middle School, Vallejo, CA

Monterey Pizza

Serves: 4   Prep time: 10 minutes, Bake: 15 minutes

- 1 thick gourmet pizza crust or Boboli pizza shell
- 4 cloves garlic
- 4 tablespoons olive oil
- 8 ounces turkey breast or chicken
- 1 (small) jar artichoke hearts, chopped
- 8 ounces Monterey jack cheese with peppers, shredded

Preheat oven to 400 degrees. Saute garlic in olive oil just until soft, about 3 minutes. Spread garlic and olive oil over pizza crust. Layer turkey or chicken over garlic and spread chopped artichokes over all. Top with shredded cheese and bake 15 minutes, until hot and bubbly.

"Quick! Easy! Add a tossed green salad and dinner is served!"

Kris Hawkins   Clovis West High School, Fresno, CA

Mushroom Quiche

Serves: 6   Prep time: 10 minutes, Microwave: 21 - 23 minutes

- 1 (9") deep dish pie crust, unbaked
- 1 teaspoon worcestershire sauce
- 1 cup Swiss cheese, grated
- 1/2 cup summer sausage, diced
- 1 teaspoon instant minced onion
- 1 (4 ounce) can sliced mushrooms, drained
- 3 eggs
- 1 cup heavy cream, or evaporated milk
- 1/2 teaspoon salt
- 1 (3 ounce) can French fried onions

Using pastry brush, spread worcestershire sauce on pie crust. Microwave at 100% power for 2 minutes; turn, microwave 2 minutes more. Sprinkle cheese, sausage, minced onion and mushrooms evenly over crust. Beat together eggs, cream and salt; pour over filling. Sprinkle French fried onions over top. Microwave at 50% power 10 minutes, turn, and microwave 7 to 9 minutes more, or until center is set. Let stand 5 minutes before serving.

Rhonda Nelson   Rancho Santa Margarita IS, Rancho Santa Margarita, CA

Parmesan Pasta

Serves: 4   Prep time: 25 minutes

- 3 cups spiral pasta
- 2 tablespoons olive oil or butter
- 3 cups zucchini, sliced
- 2 cloves garlic, minced
- salt and pepper, to taste
- 1/3 cup Parmesan cheese, grated

Cook pasta according to package directions. Meanwhile, in a large skillet over medium heat, heat oil. Add vegetables, garlic and seasonings; cook 5 to 7 minutes or until tender. Drain pasta and toss with vegetables. Sprinkle with Parmesan and toss until well coated.

"It is fun to experiment with different kinds of seasonal vegetables."

Julie Eyre   Alhambra High School, Alhambra, CA

Pasta In Tomato Cream Sauce

Serves: 4   Prep time: 15 minutes

- 8 ounces penne or other tube pasta
- 1 (14.5 ounce) can Del Monte Diced Tomatoes with Garlic & Onion
- 1/2 cup fresh basil, chopped OR 1 teaspoon dried basil
- 3/4 cup whipping cream
- 1/3 cup Parmesan cheese, grated

Cook pasta according to package directions; drain and keep warm.

Cook tomatoes over medium-high heat in skillet until thickened, about 5 minutes. Reduce heat; add basil and cream. Heat through. DO NOT BOIL. Toss with pasta and cheese. Serve immediately.

Del Monte Foods   **San Francisco, CA**

Pasta Primavera

Serves: 5   Prep time: 30 minutes

6 ounces mini lasagna noodles (or any pasta noodle)
1 cup fresh broccoli florets
3 ounces fresh mushrooms, sliced (1 cup)
$1/2$ medium yellow squash, cut into 1 $1/2$" x $1/4$" strips ($1/2$ cup)
$1/2$ medium zucchini squash, cut into 1 $1/2$" x $1/4$" strips ($1/2$ cup)
$1/2$ medium carrot, sliced ($1/2$ cup)
$1/4$ cup water
Lowfat Cream Sauce:
$1/2$ cup nonfat dry milk powder
1 $1/2$ tablespoons flour
1 large clove garlic, minced
1 teaspoon dried oregano
$1/2$ teaspoon dried basil
$1/4$ teaspoon salt
$1/4$ teaspoon pepper
1 cup water
$1/2$ cup lowfat or nonfat mozzarella cheese, shredded
Garnish: 1 tablespoon snipped fresh parsley, Parmesan cheese, freshly grated

Prepare noodles as directed on package; rinse and let stand in warm water. Meanwhile, in a large Dutch oven, combine broccoli, mushrooms, squash, carrots and $1/4$ cup water. Cover and cook on medium-low heat, stirring occasionally for 5 to 7 minutes, or until vegetables are tender crisp. DO NOT OVERCOOK. Drain; set aside. In 2 quart saucepan, combine dry milk, flour, garlic, oregano, basil, salt and pepper. Using plastic whisk, blend in remaining 1 cup water. Cook over medium-low heat, stirring frequently for 20 minutes or until sauce thickens and bubbles. Remove sauce from heat after thickened. Stir in mozzarella cheese until melted. In large mixing bowl, combine vegetables, noodles and sauce. Toss to combine. Garnish with parsley and Parmesan cheese.

Ruth Anne Mills   **Los Alisos Intermediate School, Mission Viejo, CA**

Pasta With Stir-Fry Veggies

Serves: 4   Prep time: 30 minutes

    1 package corkscrew pasta
    2 cups fresh vegetables of choice, cut into bite-sized pieces
        (broccoli, carrots, celery, onion, mushrooms, bell pepper, etc.)
    1 clove garlic, minced
    1 tablespoon butter
    1 tablespoon olive oil
    1 teaspoon salt
    $1/2$ cup fresh Parmesan cheese, grated

Cook pasta according to package directions. While pasta cooks, stir-fry vegetables and garlic in butter and olive oil. Drain noodles and add them to vegetable mixture. Heat about 1 minute. Add salt and toss. Grate cheese on top and serve.

"A good way to use excess vegetables - healthy too."

Jane Souza   **No. Monterey Co. High School, Castroville, CA**

Penne Pasta with Garlic Parmesan Sauce

Serves: 4   Prep time: 20 minutes

    16 cups water
    4 cups penne pasta
    1 teaspoon salt
    1 tablespoon olive oil
    4 cloves garlic, finely minced
    4 tablespoons butter
    4 tablespoons flour
    4 cups milk
    2 cups Romano or Parmesan cheese, grated

In a large saucepan, bring water to rolling boil. Add oil and salt; stir in pasta and boil 10 minutes, stirring often so noodles don't stick to pot. Meanwhile, in a saucepan, melt butter and saute garlic. Add the flour and cook until mixture looks like wet sand. Add milk, all at once. Heat slowly, stirring often. (It will be lumpy at first.) Two minutes before you are ready to serve, add the cheese. Do not overheat or cheese will be stringy. Serve over hot pasta.

"This rich pasta supper is especially tasty with steamed zucchini,
French bread and freshly sliced fruit."

Priscilla Burns   **Pleasant Valley High School, Chico, CA**

Penne with Tomato Sauce & Ricotta Cheese

Serves: 6   Prep time: 30 minutes

     1 pound penne, mostaccioli or other medium shaped pasta, uncooked
     1 (28 ounce) can whole plum tomatoes with basil
     $1/_2$ cup fresh basil, loosely packed
     2 (small) cloves garlic, finely chopped
     1 cup part skim ricotta cheese
     $1/_4$ cup Parmesan cheese, grated
     salt, to taste
     freshly ground pepper, to taste
     Garnish: fresh basil or parsley, chopped

Prepare pasta according to package directions. While pasta is cooking, combine tomatoes with their liquid, basil and garlic in a blender or food processor. Blend at low speed until tomatoes are completely pureed. Pour mixture into large saucepan. Heat to boiling, reduce heat and simmer 5 minutes. When pasta is done, drain well. Return pasta to cooking pot, add tomato sauce and heat over low heat until sauce is simmering and pasta is coated with sauce. Remove pot from heat and stir in ricotta and Parmesan cheese until evenly distributed. Salt and pepper to taste. Divide among serving plates and garnish, as desired.

> *"Each serving provides 275 calories; 13.6 g protein; 42.8 g. carbohydrates; 5.7 g fat; 15.9 mg. cholesterol; 345 mg. sodium."*

Betty Rabin   **Sierra Vista Junior High School, Canyon Country, CA**

Spinach Casserole

Serves: 6   Prep time: 10 minutes, Bake: 30 minutes

     2 jars marinated artichokes, drained
     2 (10 ounce) packages frozen spinach, chopped, thawed and drained
     1 (8 ounce) package cream cheese, softened
     2 tablespoons butter
     4 tablespoons milk
     1 teaspoon dehydrated onion
     $1/_2$ cup Parmesan cheese, grated

Preheat oven to 350 degrees. Place artichokes in greased 8" x 10" baking dish. Spread spinach over artichokes. In separate bowl, blend cream cheese with butter, milk and onion; spread over spinach. Sprinkle with Parmesan cheese. Cover and bake 20 minutes. Remove cover and bake 10 minutes more.

Charla Rayl   **Ivy High School, Fallbrook, CA**

Tomato Basil Pizza

Serves: 4   Prep time: 10 minutes, Bake: 15 - 20 minutes

- 1 package yeast
- 1 cup warm water
- 1 teaspoon sugar
- 1 teaspoon salt
- 1 tablespoon oil
- 2 $^1/_2$ cups flour
- 2 cups mozzarella cheese, shredded
- 1 to 2 cloves garlic, minced
- 2 tablespoons fresh Parmesan cheese, grated
- 2 tablespoons fresh basil, chopped
- 1 cup mayonnaise
- 3 Roma tomatoes, thinly sliced

Preheat oven to 350 degrees. Dissolve yeast in warm water. Stir in sugar, salt and oil. Mix in flour and knead until smooth; set aside. Combine all remaining ingredients except tomatoes and set aside. Roll out pizza dough. Spread cheese mixture over pizza dough. Place tomato slices on top. Bake 15 to 20 minutes or until golden brown.

"This tastes like a gourmet treat. Your guests will think you slaved for hours.
The pizza dough for this recipe can be used for any pizza.
It is my favorite pizza dough recipe."

Laury White   **Fallbrook High School, Fallbrook, CA**

Tortellini With Red Peppers & Prosciutto

Serves: 2 - 3   Prep time: 20 minutes

- 8 ounces tortellini
- 2 tablespoons olive oil
- 2 $^1/_2$ cups broccoli florets
- 1 red bell pepper, thinly sliced
- 1 large clove garlic, minced
- 2 ounces prosciutto, thinly sliced
- $^1/_3$ cup dry white wine
- 1 teaspoon white wine vinegar
- salt and pepper, to taste
- *Garnish:* freshly grated Parmesan cheese

Cook tortellini; drain and set aside. In large saucepan or wok, heat oil to medium-high heat. Add broccoli and red bell pepper and saute 3 to 4 minutes. Stir in garlic and prosciutto; saute 1 minute more. Add white wine and vinegar and cook 30 seconds. Season to taste with salt and pepper. Add cooked tortellini and toss 1 minute. Serve with freshly grated Parmesan cheese.

"Very fast recipe, colorful, healthy and a fresh, satisfying taste!"

Margo Olsen   **Amador Valley High School, Pleasanton, CA**

126

Vegetable Enchilada

Serves: 4 - 6   Prep time: 20 minutes, Bake: 10 minutes

6 cups assorted frozen vegetables (I use broccoli, cauliflower and carrots)
2 tablespoons oil
$^1/_8$ to $^1/_4$ teaspoon chili powder (to taste)
$^1/_8$ to $^1/_4$ teaspoon cumin (to taste)
salt and pepper, to taste
1 cup cheddar cheese, grated (divided)
1 cup Monterey jack cheese, grated (divided)
12 flour tortillas
1 jar salsa

Cook vegetables in microwave on HIGH until done, about 10 to 14 minutes. In large skillet, heat oil over medium-high heat. Quickly stir-fry vegetables; add spices, stir. Add one half cup of each cheese; stir and remove from heat. In a greased 13" x 9" pan, fill each flour tortilla with vegetable mixture and roll closed. Place seam side down in pan. Spoon salsa across top and sprinkle with remaining cheese. Bake at 350 degrees, about 10 minutes.

"This is a favorite recipe that I got from a dear friend of mine while in college. Thanks Rosie!"

Ruth Schletewitz   **Rafer Johnson Junior High School, Kingsburg, CA**

Desserts

Cakes • Cookies • Candy

10 Minute Peanut Brittle

Serves: 4   Prep time: Microwave 7 - 10 minutes

1 cup sugar
$^1/_2$ cup light corn syrup
$^1/_8$ teaspoon salt
1 to 1 $^1/_2$ cups nuts, roasted, salted
1 tablespoon margarine
1 teaspoon vanilla
1 teaspoon soda

In a 2 quart microwave casserole dish, combine sugar, corn syrup and salt. Microwave at HIGH 5 minutes. Stir in peanuts. Microwave 3 to 5 minutes, stirring after 3 minutes, until syrup and peanuts are lightly browned. Stir in margarine, vanilla and soda until light and foamy. Spread to $^1/_4$" thickness on a well-buttered cookie sheet. When cool, break into pieces.

"Delicious and much faster than the old version!"

Judy Hammann   **Mesa Junior High School, Mesa, AZ**

Almond Joy Cookies

Makes: 36   Prep time: 20 minutes, Bake: 10 - 12 minutes

1 (14 ounce) can sweetened condensed milk
2 (1 ounce) squares bittersweet chocolate
3 cups coconut, sweetened, flaked
1 teaspoon vanilla
dash salt
whole almonds

Preheat oven to 350 degrees. In top of double boiler over hot, not boiling water, stir milk and chocolate until chocolate is melted and mixture is smooth. Pour chocolate mixture over coconut. Mix with wooden spoon; add vanilla and salt. Drop by teaspoonfuls onto a cookie sheet that has been lined with parchment paper. Top each cookie with a whole almond. Bake 10 to 12 minutes, but start checking after 8 minutes, to prevent excessive browning.

"If you love the candy bar, you'll love these!"

Kathy Warren   **McClatchy High School, Sacramento, CA**

128

Piña Colada Sorbet
5 min. of preparation.
Page 144

Easy Peach Crisp
5 min. of preparation.
Page 136

Snappy Halibut Skillet
7 min. of preparation.
Page 111

Berry Crisp

Serves: 6   **Prep time: 15 minutes, Bake: 30 minutes**

1 $1/_4$ cups flour
$3/_4$ cup sugar
$3/_4$ teaspoon cinnamon
9 tablespoons butter
8 cups assorted berries, sliced strawberries, blueberries, raspberries or blackberries

Preheat oven to 375 degrees. Combine flour, sugar and cinnamon in a bowl. Blend butter in with a pastry cutter until crumbly. Butter bottom of baking pan. Place berries in pan and sprinkle with crumb mixture, covering all. Bake 30 minutes.

"Serve with vanilla ice cream. Easy and delicious!"

Yolanda Carlos   **Victor Valley High School, Victorville, CA**

Big Tin Chocolate Cake

Serves: 12 - 18   **Prep time: 15 minutes, Bake: 20 minutes**

Cake:
2 cups flour
2 cups sugar
1 cup margarine
$1/_4$ cup cocoa
1 cup water
$1/_2$ cup buttermilk or sour milk
2 eggs, beaten
1 teaspoon baking soda
1 teaspoon vanilla
Frosting:
$1/_3$ cup margarine
$1/_4$ cup cocoa
5 tablespoons milk
1 pound powdered sugar, sifted
Garnish: walnuts, chopped (optional)

Preheat oven to 400 degrees. Sift flour and sugar together. Bring margarine, cocoa and water to a boil; pour over dry ingredients and mix well. Mix buttermilk, eggs, baking soda and vanilla together well. Mix into other ingredients. Spread into a jelly roll pan and bake 20 minutes. During last five minutes of baking time, prepare frosting. Bring margarine, cocoa and milk to a boil. Mix in powdered sugar. Let cake cook cool slightly and spread frosting over top. Be careful, or it will spill over if too warm. Sprinkle nuts over cake, if desired.

"This is the most frequently asked for dessert at our house. It is the number one favorite birthday cake for family members. It freezes very well also!"

Kathleen Fresquez   **Mountain View High School, El Monte, CA**

Black Cherry Cheese Pie

Serves: 6 - 8   Prep time: 10 minutes, Chill: 20 minutes

  1 (small) package black cherry jello
  1 cup hot water
  $1/2$ cup ice cubes
  1 $1/2$ pints whipping cream
  1 (3 ounce) package cream cheese, softened
  1 (9") graham cracker crust
  1 large can pitted black cherries, drained, cut in half

Mix jello with hot water; stir until completely dissolved. Stir in ice cubes until melted. Refrigerate until partially set, about 20 minutes. Meanwhile, whip cream with cream cheese and pour into pie shell. Spread with jello. Top with cherries. Refrigerate until ready to eat.

Donna Fippin   **Bret Harte Union High School, Altaville, CA**

Blintz Soufflé

Serves: 12   Prep time: 10 minutes, Bake: 35 minutes

  12 blintzes (2 packages), thawed
  6 eggs
  4 tablespoons butter, melted
  $1/2$ (small) can frozen orange juice concentrate
  1 tablespoon vanilla
  3 tablespoon sugar
  $1/2$ teaspoon salt
  2 cups sour cream

Preheat oven to 350 degrees. Arrange blintzes in a buttered 9" x 13" dish. In blender, mix all other ingredients; blend well. Pour over top of blintzes. Bake on middle rack 35 minutes or until a knife inserted in center comes out clean.

Lynda Ruth   **La Mirada High School, La Mirada, CA**

Brownie Pie

Serves: 4 - 6   Prep time: 5 minutes, Bake: 15 minutes

  nonstick cooking spray
  1 egg
  $1/2$ cup sugar
  $1/4$ cup butter or margarine
  $1/4$ cup flour
  2 tablespoons cocoa powder
  $1/2$ teaspoon vanilla
  $1/4$ cup nuts, chopped (optional)

Preheat oven to 325 degrees. Spray an 8" pie pan with nonstick cooking spray. Place all ingredients into a bowl and mix. Spread evenly into pie pan. Bake 15 minutes. Cut into pie wedges and serve with ice cream or whipped cream.

Carol Steele   La Paz Intermediate School, Mission Viejo, CA

Brownie Sundae
Serves: 8   Prep time: 10 minutes, Freeze: 20 minutes
  1 package brownie mix, prepared
  $^1/_2$ gallon ice cream, any flavor, softened
  1 jar fudge topping

Prepare brownie mix according to package directions; cool. Spread softened ice cream over brownies. Freeze until firm. Spread ice cream with fudge topping and serve.

Brenda Umbro   Orange Glen High School, Escondido, CA

Butterscotch Pecan Cookies
Serves: 8   Prep time: 10 minutes, Bake: 10 - 12 minutes
  1 package butter recipe cake mix
  1 (3.4 ounce) box instant butterscotch pudding mix
  $^1/_4$ cup flour
  $^3/_4$ cup vegetable oil
  1 egg
  1 cup pecans, chopped

Preheat oven to 350 degrees. In a mixing bowl, combine first five ingredients; mix well. Stir in pecans. Dough will be crumbly. Roll dough into 1" balls. Place 2" apart on greased baking sheet. Bake 10 to 12 minutes, until golden brown.

Jeanette Atkinson   Brinley Middle School, Las Vegas, NV

Cherries In The Snow
Serves: 8 - 12   Prep time: 15 minutes, Chill: 2 hours
  2 (loaf style) angel food cakes
  1 (8 ounce) package cream cheese
  1 cup powdered sugar
  1 (12 ounce) container Cool Whip
  1 (21 ounce) can cherry pie filling

Cut each cake into 8 slices. Combine cream cheese and powdered sugar in a bowl and beat at medium speed until smooth; set aside. To assemble the cake, spread half of the Cool Whip in the bottom of a 9" x 13" pan. Arrange 8 slices of cake on the whipped topping and press lightly. Spread cake with cream cheese mixture. Arrange remaining cake pieces on top of cream cheese mixture. Spread with remaining whipped topping. Spoon cherry pie filling over top. Chill 2 hours or until ready to serve.

Toni Purtill   Basic High School, Henderson, NV

Cherry Fluff

Serves: 12 - 16   **Prep time: 15 minutes**

10 graham crackers, crushed
$1/_3$ cup margarine, melted
$1/_3$ cup sugar
2 cans cherry pie filling
1 can crushed pineapple, drained
1 large container Cool Whip
1 can sweetened condensed milk
1 cup pecans

Preheat oven to 350 degrees. Mix together crushed graham crackers, melted margarine and sugar. Press into bottom of a 9" x 13" pan. Bake 10 minutes; cool. Mix together pie filling, pineapple, Cool Whip and condensed milk; pour into cooled crust. Sprinkle with pecans. Refrigerate 4 to 24 hours. Cut into squares to serve.

Toni Purtill   **Basic High School, Henderson, NV**

Chocolate Chip Cookie Pizza

Serves: 8   **Prep time: 15 minutes, Bake: 12 - 15 minutes**

1 (18 ounce) roll refrigerated chocolate chip cookie dough
2 to 3 (5 ounce) cups chocolate pudding (more or less, as desired)
$1/_2$ cup plain yogurt
$1/_3$ cup peanut butter
Toppings: 2 sliced bananas, mini chocolate chips, chopped peanuts, walnuts, raisins, coconut, marshmallows or broken candy bars.
Garnish: maraschino cherries

Preheat oven to 350 degrees. Line a 12" pizza pan with foil. Press cookie dough evenly into pan. Bake 12 to 15 minutes until golden. Remove from oven and cool on rack. Meanwhile, stir together chocolate pudding, yogurt and peanut butter. Spread mixture over cooled cookie crust. Select toppings and sprinkle evenly over pudding mixture. Garnish with cherries in middle. Cut into wedges and serve immediately. NOTE: A can of chocolate frosting may be substituted for the chocolate pudding/yogurt/peanut butter mixture.

Betty Byrne   **Vaca Peña Middle School, Vacaville, CA**

Chocolate Graham Cookie Bars

Makes: 24 bars   **Prep time: 10 minutes, Bake: 5 minutes**

12 double chocolate graham crackers
1 cup butter
1 cup light brown sugar
1 (11.75 ounce) package milk chocolate chips
1 cup pecans, chopped

Preheat oven to 400 degrees. Line a jelly roll pan or metal cookie sheet with foil. Place graham crackers on foil. In a saucepan, melt butter with brown sugar. Bring to a boil and boil 3 minutes, stirring constantly. (It should become thick.) Pour over crackers and spread evenly. Bake 5 minutes, watching carefully so they don't burn. Remove from oven and sprinkle chocolate chips over top; spread evenly. Sprinkle chopped pecans over. Cut into squares while still warm.

"This is so simple and SO delicious. It tastes almost like Almond Roca bars."

Millie Deeton   Ayala High School, Chino Hills, CA

Chocolate Orange Mousse
Serves: 6   Prep time: 15 minutes

  1 cup heavy cream
  1 (8 ounce) package cream cheese, softened
  $3/_4$ cup sugar
  $1/_4$ cup unsweetened cocoa powder
  1 tablespoon orange zest, grated

In a medium bowl with electric mixer on high speed, beat cream to stiff peaks; set aside. In another bowl, beat cream cheese and sugar together on medium speed until smooth. With the mixer on low speed, beat in cocoa powder and orange zest. Gently beat in half of the whipped cream. Remove mixer and fold in remaining whipped cream by hand. Pour into six dessert dishes and serve or refrigerate.

Nan Paul   Grant Middle School, Escondido, CA

Chocolate Peanut Butter Balls
Makes: 5 dozen   Prep time: 30 minutes

  2 $1/_2$ cups Rice Krispies
  3 cups powdered sugar
  1 $1/_2$ cups peanut butter
  1 cube butter
  1 (12 ounce) package chocolate chips
  $1/_4$ bar paraffin wax, grated
  wooden skewers

Mix Rice Krispies and powdered sugar lightly. In a saucepan, melt together peanut butter and butter until mixture becomes liquid, stirring until thoroughly combined. Pour over Rice Krispies mixture a little at a time until evenly coated. Roll into balls the size of small walnuts. Place on cookie sheet and chill until firm. Meanwhile, in top of double boiler over hot, not boiling water, melt chocolate chips with paraffin wax, stirring constantly until mixture becomes liquid and no lumps are left. Pierce a peanut butter ball slightly with a wooden skewer. Dip into chocolate and tap skewer on side of pan so excess

133

chocolate can drip off. Place on waxed paper. Drizzle melted chocolate over hole to give finished look. Chill.

"This recipe was from my high school teacher from Upland, Mrs. Rhodes."

Cyndy Riede   **South High School, Torrance, CA**

Chocolate Yummies

Makes: 3 dozen   **Prep time: 15 minutes**

1 (6 ounce) package chocolate chips
$^1/_3$ cup butter or margarine
16 large marshmallows
$^1/_2$ teaspoon vanilla
1 cup coconut
2 cups rolled oats

In a large saucepan, melt chocolate chips, butter and marshmallows, stirring until smooth. Remove from heat. Stir in vanilla, coconut and oats. Mix thoroughly. Drop by teaspoonfuls on waxed paper. Let cool.

"This is a quick treat to make. Also, easy for kids too, with supervision."

Maria Montemagni   **Mt. Whitney High School, Visalia, CA**

Churros

Serves: 6 - 8   **Prep time: 30 minutes**

1 cup water
$^1/_4$ teaspoon salt
1 teaspoon sugar
$^1/_2$ cup butter or margarine
1 cup flour
4 eggs
oil, for frying
Topping: $^3/_4$ cup sugar, mixed with 1 tablespoon cinnamon

Combine water, salt, 1 teaspoon sugar and butter in a large saucepan. Cook over low heat, stirring until butter melts. Increase heat and bring mixture to a rolling boil. Add flour, all at once, then remove pan from heat. Beat with wooden spoon until mixture is smooth and thick and pulls away from sides of pan. Add eggs, one at a time, beating well after each addition. If time allows, set aside to cool. Using a deep fryer or electric skillet, heat enough oil to reach depth of 1 $^1/_2$" in pan to 375 degrees. Spoon $^1/_2$ of dough into pastry bag fitted with large star tip. Squeeze ribbon of dough 7" to 8" in length into hot oil. Slice off dough with sharp knife or scissors. Cook until well browned. Remove with slotted spoon and drain on paper towels. Sprinkle with cinnamon sugar.

Jan Hirth   **Saddleback High School, Santa Ana, CA**

Double Chocolate Chip Cookies

Makes: 2 - 3 dozen — Prep time: 10 minutes, Bake: 11 minutes

1 chocolate fudge cake mix
$1/2$ cup flour
$1/2$ cup oil or melted butter
2 eggs, beaten
1 (6 ounce) chocolate chips
$1/2$ cup nuts, optional

Preheat oven to 375 degrees. Mix all ingredients together well. Drop onto lightly greased cookie sheet and bake 9 to 11 minutes.

"My grandmother gave me this recipe.My husband's favorite cookie."

Kathy Sandoz — Mesa Junior High School, Mesa, AZ

Easy Apple Pie

Serves: 6 - 8 — Prep time: 20 minutes, Bake: 7 minutes

3 green apples, sliced
1 teaspoon lemon juice
1 tablespoon sugar
2 teaspoons cinnamon
$3/4$ cup butter
$3/4$ cup sugar
2 eggs, beaten
1 cup flour

Preheat oven to 375 degrees. Mix together first 4 ingredients until all apple slices are coated. Pour into pie tin. Melt butter in saucepan and cook until golden brown in color. Remove from heat; slowly add sugar, eggs and flour. Pour over apples and bake 7 minutes.

"Serve with ice cream or sliced cheddar cheese. You'll be a hit!"

Carol Fleming — Rancho Cucamonga High School, Rancho Cucamonga, CA

Easy French Apple Pie

Serves: 8 — Prep time: 20 minutes

1 (3 $1/8$ ounce) package instant vanilla pudding mix, prepared
1 (16 ounce) can apple pie filling
1 (8" or 9") baked pie crust
Garnish: sweetened whipped cream or non-dairy topping, nutmeg, cinnamon

Prepare vanilla pudding mix according to package directions. Spoon apple pie filling into baked pie crust. Spread vanilla pudding over apple filling. Top with whipped cream piped through pastry bag using rose tube, if desired. Sprinkle with cinnamon or nutmeg.

Carol Goddard — Alhambra High School, Alhambra, CA

135

Easy Peach Crisp

Serves: 6   Prep time: 5 minutes, Bake: 15 minutes

    2 (15.25 ounce) cans Del Monte Sliced Peaches, drained
    2 (1.6 ounce) packages cinnamon and spice instant oatmeal, uncooked
    $1/_3$ cup flour
    $1/_2$ cup walnuts, chopped
    $1/_3$ cup butter, melted

Preheat oven to 425 degrees. Pour peaches into lightly buttered 2 quart baking dish. Combine instant oatmeal with flour and nuts in a bowl; stir in butter. Sprinkle over peaches. Bake 15 minutes or until golden brown. Serve over ice cream, if desired.

Del Monte Foods   **San Francisco, CA**

Four Minute Brownie Pie

Serves: 8   Prep time: 10 minutes, Bake: 30 minutes

    2 eggs
    1 cup sugar
    $1/_2$ cup butter, softened
    $1/_2$ cup flour
    4 tablespoons cocoa
    1 teaspoon vanilla
    dash salt
    $1/_2$ cup walnuts, chopped
    Garnish: whipped or ice cream

Preheat oven to 325 degrees. Place eggs, sugar, butter, flour, cocoa, vanilla and salt in small mixer bowl; beat 4 minutes. Stir in nuts and pour into greased 8" pie pan. Bake 30 minutes or until done. Will settle like meringue when cool. Cut into wedges and serve with whipped or ice cream.

Pam Ford   **Temecula Valley High School, Temecula, CA**

Holiday Peanut Brittle

Makes: 3 dozen   Prep time: 20 minutes

    $1/_2$ cup boiling water
    1 $1/_2$ cups sugar
    $1/_2$ cup corn syrup
    2 cups Spanish peanuts, raw
    2 tablespoons butter
    1 $1/_2$ teaspoons baking soda

Bring water to a boil; stir in sugar and corn syrup and stir until dissolved. Boil on medium heat to 235 degrees (use candy thermometer). Stir in peanuts and butter. Stir constantly until mixture reaches 300 degrees. Remove from heat and stir in baking soda. Pour immediately onto a well-greased cookie sheet; spread thin.

Cool completely and break into pieces to serve.

Diana Lee   **David A. Brown Middle School, Wildomar, CA**

Hopscotch Crunchies

Makes: 3 dozen   **Prep time: 20 minutes**

1 cup peanut butter
1 package butterscotch chips
4 cups chow mein noodles
1 cup peanuts (optional)
2 cups miniature marshmallows

In top of double boiler over hot, not boiling water, melt peanut butter and butterscotch chips, stirring occasionally. Place noodles, peanuts and marshmallows in large bowl. Pour melted mixture over noodle mixture and stir well, until evenly coated. Drop by teaspoonfuls onto waxed paper lined cookie sheet. Chill until set.

Sue Ogden   **San Clemente High School, San Clemente, CA**

Ice Cream Pie

Serves: 4 - 6   **Prep time: 10 minutes**

$^1/_3$ cup peanut butter
$^1/_3$ cup white corn syrup
3 cups Rice Krispies cereal
$^1/_2$ gallon vanilla ice cream

Mix peanut butter with corn syrup. Stir in cereal and stir to mix thoroughly. Press into bottom of 9" pie pan to form a crust. Fill with slightly softened ice cream and freeze until firm. To serve, let stand at room temperature about 20 minutes.

"Mother always gets requests for this recipe. Easy and yummy too!"

Jean Hanson   **Red Bluff Union High School, Red Bluff, CA**

Indoor S'Mores

Serves: 12   **Prep time: 15 minutes**

$^1/_2$ cup chocolate chips
12 long graham crackers, broken in half
12 marshmallows

Preheat oven to 400 degrees. Cover a cookie sheet with foil. Melt chocolate chips in microwave on HIGH for 1 $^1/_2$ to 2 minutes. Blend until smooth. Spread melted chocolate on half of the graham crackers. Place a marshmallow on top of each chocolate covered cracker. Place these crackers on the foiled cookie sheet. Bake 3 minutes, or until marshmallows are puffed and browned. Now top with remaining crackers, pressing down to smash marshmallow.

Joanne Fial   **East Middle School, Downey, CA**

John & Brenda's Toffee Popcorn

Makes: 1 ¹/₂ gallons   **Prep time: 15 minutes**

  7 quarts popped corn
  ¹/₂ cup Karo syrup
  2 cups brown sugar
  1 cup margarine
  1 teaspoon baking soda

Place popped corn in large brown paper bag. In saucepan, bring Karo syrup, brown sugar and margarine to a boil; boil 5 minutes, stirring constantly. Remove from heat; add baking soda; stir. Pour over popcorn and stir to mix. Roll down sides of paper bag; microwave 1 minute; stir. Dump onto waxed paper to cool.

"This is a favorite of the 'Tough Parenting Network'. Great for meetings and gifts."

Mary M. Rector   **Valley High School, Las Vegas, NV**

Key Lime Pie

Serves: 8   **Prep time: 5 minutes, Bake: 15 minutes**

  ¹/₂ cup key lime juice
  1 (14 ounce) sweetened condensed milk
  3 egg yolks
  1 (9") prepared graham cracker crust
  Garnish: Cool Whip, lime slices

Preheat oven to 350 degrees. Pour lime juice, milk and egg yolks into a blender; blend until smooth. Pour into pie crust. Bake 15 minutes. Allow to stand 10 minutes before refrigerating. Garnish with Cool Whip and lime slices.

"A friend I teach with serves this often when in a time pinch for a dessert."

Vicki Giannetti   **Foothill High School, Sacramento, CA**

Lemon Cookies

Makes: 4 dozen   **Prep time: 10 minutes, Bake: 15 minutes**

  1 package lemon cake mix
  1 (8 ounce) carton Cool Whip
  1 whole egg
  1 pound powdered sugar

Preheat oven to 350 degrees. Mix together cake mix, Cool Whip, and egg until thoroughly blended. Chill thoroughly, 3 to 4 hours. After chilling, scoop up 1 teaspoonful at a time, and roll into balls; roll balls in powdered sugar and place on cookie sheet. Bake 12 to 15 minutes. Cool and enjoy.

"For a tasty variation, I have also used devil's food and spice cake mixes."

Vicki Pearl   **Giano Intermediate School, La Puente, CA**

Magical Apple Pie

Serves: 8   Prep time: 10 minutes, Bake: 25 - 30 minutes

  1 egg
  $3/4$ cup sugar
  $1/2$ cup all-purpose flour
  1 teaspoon baking powder
  pinch salt
  1 medium tart apple, peeled, diced
  $1/2$ cup raisins
  Garnish: whipped or ice cream

Preheat oven to 350 degrees. In a mixing bowl, beat egg. Add sugar, flour, baking powder and salt. Stir in apple and raisins. Spread into a greased 9" pie plate. Bake 25 to 30 minutes or until golden brown and toothpick inserted near center comes out clean. Garnish with whipped or ice cream.

> *"A unique pie because it forms it's own crust on top as it bakes, it has a chewy cake-like consistency. It's inexpensive too, just 13 cents a slice!"*

Connie Sweet   **Rim Of The World High School, Lake Arrowhead, CA**

Microwave Caramel Corn

Makes: 1 gallon   Prep time: 15 minutes

  1 cup brown sugar
  $1/2$ cup butter or margarine
  $1/3$ cup white corn syrup
  $1/2$ teaspoon salt
  $1/2$ teaspoon baking soda
  4 quarts popped corn

In a 1 $1/2$ quart microwave dish, stir together brown sugar, butter or margarine, corn syrup and salt. Microwave on HIGH 2 minutes; stir. Microwave on HIGH 2 minutes more. Stir in baking soda. Pour mixture over popped corn in large brown paper grocery bag. Shake well to coat. Place bag in microwave and cook on HIGH 2 minutes. Shake bag and return to microwave for an additional 1 $1/2$ minutes. Pour onto waxed paper to cool. Stir to keep kernels separated. Caution! Mixture will be very hot!

> *"Great for lab or home use. If you like Cracker Jacks, you will love this!"*

April Rosendahl   **Chino High School, Chino, CA**

Microwave Carrot Cake

Serves: 6   Prep time: 15 minutes, Microwave: 15 minutes

Cake:
1 $1/2$ cups sugar
1 cup oil
1 teaspoon vanilla
3 eggs
1 $1/2$ cups unsifted flour
$3/4$ teaspoon salt
1 $1/2$ teaspoons baking soda
2 $1/2$ teaspoons cinnamon
1 $1/4$ cups raw carrots, grated
$1/2$ cup walnuts, chopped
1 (8 ounce) can crushed pineapple, drained
Frosting:
1 pound powdered sugar
1 (8 ounce) package cream cheese
6 tablespoons butter
2 teaspoons vanilla

Mix sugar, oil and vanilla in large mixing bowl. Add eggs and beat well. In separate bowl, combine flour, salt, baking soda and cinnamon; stir into creamed mixture. Fold in carrots, walnuts and pineapple. Pour batter into 12" x 7" microwave dish which has been greased on the bottom only. Cook in microwave on HIGH 15 minutes, turning $1/4$ turn every 4 minutes. Cool; prepare frosting. Place sugar in 2 quart casserole. Add cream cheese, butter and vanilla. Cook in microwave on HIGH 1 minute, just until ingredients can be beaten together. Beat with electric mixer until fluffy. Frost cooled cake.

"A great dessert. I use a Cuisinart for the carrots and lower fat cream cheese."

Faye Nielsen   **Rosemead High School, Rosemead, CA**

Monkey Bread

Serves: 4 - 5   Prep time: 5 minutes, Microwave: 3 - 4 minutes

$1/4$ cup margarine
$1/2$ cup brown sugar
2 tablespoons water
$1/2$ cup walnuts, chopped (optional)
1 package refrigerator biscuits

In a round microwave dish, melt margarine, brown sugar and water in microwave on HIGH, about 45 seconds. Sprinkle nuts into mixture (if using) and top with biscuits, placed side by side. Microwave on HIGH 3 to 4 minutes, or until biscuits are cooked through. Let stand 1 minute before serving.

Kathie Hogen   **Hendrix Junior High School, Chandler, AZ**

"No-Bake" Chinese Chocolate Cookies

Makes: 12 - 15 cookies   Prep time: 15 minutes, Chill: 10 - 15 minutes

    1 cup chocolate chips
    $^1/_2$ cup butterscotch chips
    $^1/_4$ cup peanut butter
    $^1/_2$ teaspoon vanilla
    2 cups Chinese noodles
    $^1/_2$ cup peanuts (optional)

Melt chocolate and peanut butter chips with peanut butter over low heat on top of stove or in microwave on 50% power. Stir in vanilla and noodles. If desired, stir in peanuts. Drop by tablespoonfuls on waxed paper lined baking trays. Refrigerate 10 to 15 minutes until set.

"This quick cookie recipe is a favorite of my middle school students.
It's convenient to mix, 'bake' and eat in a 50 minute class period!"

Shirley Blough   **Hillside Middle School, Simi Valley, CA**

Oreo O's Bars

Makes: 18   Prep time: 15 minutes

    $^1/_2$ stick butter or margarine ($^1/_4$ cup)
    1 (10.5 ounce) package miniature marshmallows (6 cups)
    8 cups Post Oreo O's cereal

Microwave butter in a 4 quart microwave bowl on HIGH for 45 seconds or until melted. Add marshmallows; mix to coat. Microwave 1 $^1/_2$ minutes or until marshmallows are melted and smooth, stirring after 45 seconds. Add cereal; mix to coat well. Press firmly into a greased, foil-lined 13" x 9" pan. Cool; cut into rectangles. To make chocolate *Oreo O Bars:* prepare as directed, melting 2 squares of Baker's semi-sweet baking chocolate with the butter.

"This is easy, fun and absolutely yummy!
My Foods students love making this. Younger children enjoy it too!"

Elizabeth Ward   **Taft Union High School, Taft, CA**

"Oreos"

Makes: 20 cookies   Prep time: 20 minutes, Bake: 7 - 10 minutes

    Cookies:
    1 package devil's food cake mix
    1 egg, slightly beaten
    1 cube margarine, melted
    Cream Cheese Filling:
    $^1/_3$ cup margarine
    3 ounces cream cheese
    3 cups powdered sugar, divided
    1 $^1/_2$ teaspoons vanilla
    1 $^1/_2$ tablespoons light cream

Preheat oven to 350 degrees. *Prepare cookies:* Mix together cake mix, egg and melted margarine. Form into balls the size of walnuts and place on ungreased cookie sheet. Bake 7 to 10 minutes. Allow to cool completely. *Prepare filling:* Cream margarine and cream cheese; gradually add 1 $^1/_2$ cups powdered sugar blending well. Beat in vanilla, remaining 1 $^1/_2$ cups powdered sugar, and enough cream to make filling spreading consistency. Spread filing between cooled cookies and enjoy!

Marleigh Williams   **Corning High School, Corning, CA**

Peanut Butter Bars
Makes: 36   Prep time: 5 minutes, Bake: 6 - 8 minutes

  1 $^3/_4$ cups graham cracker crumbs
  1 $^3/_4$ cups peanut butter
  1 $^1/_2$ cubes butter, melted
  2 cups powdered sugar
  2 cups semi-sweet chocolate chips (12 ounce bag)

Preheat oven to 350 degrees. Mix together all but the chocolate chips and pat into 9" x 13" pan. Sprinkle chocolate chips on top. Bake 6 to 8 minutes. After removing from oven, spread melted chocolate chips to cover the top. Refrigerate until chips are hardened.

"This recipe was given to me by my former student, Margie Briggs, who is now a paraprofessional aïde at our school."

Nancy Jordan   **Merced High School, Merced, CA**

Peanut Butter Brownies
Makes: 3 dozen   Prep time: 15 minutes, Bake: 30 - 35 minutes

  1 $^1/_2$ cups sugar
  $^1/_2$ cup margarine, softened
  3 eggs
  $^1/_2$ cup peanut butter
  1 cup flour
  $^1/_2$ teaspoon baking powder
  $^1/_2$ teaspoon salt
  1 teaspoon vanilla
  1 cup chocolate chips
  1 cup peanuts, chopped (optional)

Preheat oven to 350 degrees. Cream together sugar and margarine. Add eggs and peanut butter and mix well. Blend in dry ingredients until well mixed. Add vanilla. Fold in chocolate chips and peanuts then spread in a greased 9" x 13" pan. Bake 30 to 35 minutes, or until lightly browned.

"These bars disappear quickly and are simple to make."

Wendy Johnson   **Temecula Valley High School, Temecula, CA**

Peanut Butter Cookies

Makes: 12   **Prep time: 10 minutes, Bake: 10 - 12 minutes**

   1 cup peanut butter
   1 cup sugar
   1 egg

Preheat oven to 350 degrees. Mix ingredients together thoroughly.
Roll into 1" balls and place 2" apart on ungreased cookie sheet. Press
each ball with a fork, dipped in sugar. Bake 10 to 12 minutes. Let cool
2 to 4 minutes on cookie sheet. Remove to cool on rack.

*"These cookies must cool 2 to 4 minutes on the cookie sheet
so they will keep their shape. If not, they crumble."*

Patty Stroming   **Mitchell Senior Elementary, Atwater, CA**

Peanut Butter S'Mores

Serves: 4   **Prep time: 20 minutes**

   4 Oreo chocolate sandwich cookies
   3 tablespoons creamy peanut butter
   8 squares graham crackers
   1 tablespoon hot fudge sauce
   $1/4$ cup miniature marshmallows

Put cookies in plastic bag; break into pieces and set aside. Spread 1
teaspoon peanut butter on one side of each graham cracker squares.
Using 4 squares, top peanut butter with 1 tablespoon cookie crumbs,
$3/4$ teaspoon hot fudge sauce and 4 to 5 mini marshmallows. Top with
remaining graham cracker squares, peanut butter side down,
pressing gently to form sandwiches. Place on microwave plate and
microwave on HIGH for 20 to 30 seconds or until heated through.
Serve warm.

Gale Hooper   **Casa Roble High School, Orangevale, CA**

Pecan Fruit Streusel

Serves: 8 - 10   **Prep time: 15 minutes, Bake: 30 - 40 minutes**

   2 to 4 cups apples, peeled and sliced
   2 cups blueberries, fresh or frozen
   2 cups blackberries, fresh or frozen
   1 to 2 cups raspberries, fresh or frozen
   $3/4$ cup brown sugar
   $1/2$ cup flour
   $1/2$ cup oats
   $1 1/2$ teaspoons cinnamon
   $1/4$ cup firm butter or margarine
   $1/2$ cup pecans, coarsely chopped

Preheat oven to 375 degrees. In a greased 13" x 9" x 2" baking pan,
layer apples and berries. In another bowl, cut together brown sugar,

flour, oats, cinnamon and nuts until crumbly. Sprinkle over fruit. Bake 30 to 40 minutes, until fruit is tender and bubbly. Serve warm or cold. NOTE: This can be made ahead and baked fresh. Also, you can add any combination of fruit... fresh, frozen or canned.

"Great for breakfast, lunch or dinner."

Judi Topp   **A.B. Miller High School, Fontana, CA**

Peppermint Crunch
Makes: 1 pound   Prep time: 15 minutes, Chill: 15 - 20 minutes

    30 peppermint candies
    1 (12 ounce) package white chocolate chips
    2 tablespoons shortening

Unwrap candies and place in a 1 gallon ziploc bag. Use a meat mallet to crush candies; set aside. In large saucepan, place white chocolate chips and shortening. Melt mixture over very low heat, stirring often. When completely melted, remove from heat. Stir in crushed peppermint candies. Spread onto a jelly roll pan. Refrigerate 15 to 20 minutes. Break into pieces and serve.

"Swirl 1/2 cup melted chocolate chips into mixture before refrigerating."

Beth Guerrero   **Selma High School, Selma, CA**

Piña Colada Sorbet
Serves: 3   Prep time: 5 minutes, Freeze: 24 hours

    1 (15.5 ounce) Del Monte Pineapple in Heavy Syrup
    2 1/2 tablespoons coconut milk, well chilled
    1/2 tablespoon rum or 1/2 teaspoon rum extract

Place unopened can of fruit in freezer until solid (approximately 24 hours; can may bulge slightly). Submerge unopened frozen can in very hot tap water for 1 minute. Open can and pour any thawed syrup into food processor bowl (**not recommended for blenders or mini-food processors**). Remove frozen fruit from can; carefully cut into 8 chunks. Place frozen fruit chunks into food processor; add coconut milk and rum. Process until smooth; scraping blade as needed. Serve immediately or spoon into freezer container and freeze until ready to serve. NOTE: To double recipe, process in 2 separate batches. For firmer sorbet, freeze 1 to 2 hours prior to serving.

Del Monte Foods   **San Francisco, CA**

Praline Graham Cookies

Serves: 5 - 6   Prep time: 15 minutes, Bake: 12 minutes

    10 - 12 graham crackers
    1 cup butter
    $1/_2$ cup sugar
    1 cup nuts, chopped

Preheat oven to 350 degrees. Separate graham crackers and lay in a jelly roll pan. In a saucepan, combine butter and sugar. Bring to a boil for 3 minutes. Spread or pour over crackers and sprinkle with chopped nuts. Bake 12 minutes. Separate and cool on waxed paper.

Pamela Campion   **Dublin High School, Dublin, CA**

Raspberry Delight

Serves: 8 - 10   Prep time: 15 minutes, Freeze: 15 minutes

    $1/_2$ gallon vanilla ice cream
    $1/_2$ gallon raspberry sherbet
    3 bananas, sliced
    1 can raspberries, with juice
    $1/_2$ to 1 cup pecans or walnuts, chopped

Slightly soften ice cream and sherbet. Slice bananas, mix with raspberries & nuts. Mix all ingredients together. Refreeze. Serve soft.

Paula Schaefer   **Garside Middle School, Las Vegas, NV**

Shirley's Brownies

Serves: 12   Prep time: 5 minutes, Bake: 25 - 30 minutes

    2 cups milk
    1 (6 ounce) package instant chocolate pudding
    1 box yellow cake mix
    1 cup chocolate chips

Preheat oven to 350 degrees. Combine milk with pudding mix; add cake mix. Spread into a greased and floured 13" x 9" pan. Sprinkle with chocolate chips. Bake 20 to 25 minutes.

Linda Hsieh   **Rowland High School, Rowland Heights, CA**

Strawberries Romanoff

Serves: 8   Prep time: 15 minutes

    $1/_4$ cup + 2 tablespoons sugar, divided
    $1/_4$ cup + 2 tablespoons Grand Marnier, divided
    4 cups whole strawberries, hulled
    1 cup whipping cream
    $1/_8$ teaspoon ground cinnamon
    $1/_3$ cup sour cream
    3 tablespoons almonds, chopped

Combine $1/_4$ cup sugar and $1/_4$ cup Grand Marnier in a large bowl; stir until sugar dissolves. Add strawberries, toss gently and set aside. Beat whipping cream until foamy, gradually adding 2 tablespoons sugar, 2 tablespoons Grand Marnier and cinnamon; beat until soft peaks form. Fold in sour cream. Spoon strawberries with syrup into serving dishes. Top each with dollop of cream mixture. Sprinkle with nuts.

"For a lowfat treat, just combine $1/4$ cup sugar, $1/4$ cup Grand Marnier and strawberries in a bowl and garnish with freshly grated black pepper. Delicious!"

Joye Cantrell   **Rialto High School, Rialto, CA**

Sugar Free Banana Cream Pie
Serves: 6   Prep time: 30 minutes

   7 large graham crackers
   3 tablespoons margarine, melted
   1 (small) package vanilla or banana cream pudding mix
   1 $3/4$ cup milk
   1 cup whipped cream
   2 bananas

Process graham crackers in food processor until they are crumbs. Add melted margarine, mixing with a fork. Reserve 2 tablespoons mixture and press remainder into pie plate; chill. Prepare pudding using milk. Fold in whipped cream. Slice bananas into cooled crust; pour filling over crust, sprinkle with reserved topping and chill until ready to serve.

Pat Peck   **Folsom High School, Folsom, CA**

Yummy Fudge
Makes: 1 pound   Prep time: 10 minutes, Microwave: 2 minutes

   1 cube margarine or butter
   1 pound powdered sugar
   $1/4$ cup nonfat milk
   $1/2$ cup cocoa
   1 cup walnuts, chopped
   1 teaspoon vanilla

In a large glass bowl, melt margarine or butter in microwave. Stir in powdered sugar, milk and cocoa and stir well. Cook in microwave on HIGH 2 minutes. Add walnuts and vanilla and stir to thicken, beating well. Pour into a 9" x 9" square pan. Cool completely.

"Our Student Services Secretary, Kathleen Crofford, shared this quick, delicious recipe with us prior to the Christmas break."

Judith Huffman   **Mariposa County High School, Mariposa, CA**

Yummy Mock Toffee

Serves: 10 - 12   Prep time: 15 minutes, Chill: 15 minutes

    1 cup brown sugar
    1 cup butter (2 cubes)
    nonstick cooking spray
    35 saltines (approximate)
    1 (12 ounce) package chocolate chips
    $1/_2$ cup walnuts, chopped

Preheat oven to 400 degrees. Melt butter and sugar together in saucepan. Bring to a boil and boil 3 minutes, without stirring. While mixture is boiling, spray a 10" x 15" jelly roll pan with nonstick cooking spray. Line the pan with saltines. After sugar mixture has boiled 3 minutes, pour over crackers, covering all. Bake 5 minutes. Remove from oven and sprinkle chocolate chips over top. Smooth out as chips melt. Sprinkle chopped nuts evenly over top and chill in refrigerator until firm. Break into pieces and enjoy!

"Try this toffee. It is so delicious, no one will dream it is so easy to make. Everyone loves it!"

Lura Staffanson   **Centennial High School, Corona, CA**

Dad's Chocolate Cherry Cake

Serves: 8 - 12   Prep time: 15 minutes, Bake: 60 minutes

    Cake:
    1 package Betty Crocker fudge cake mix
    1 (21 ounce) can cherry pie filling
    $1/_2$ teaspoon almond extract
    1 teaspoon vanilla
    $1/_2$ cup water
    2 eggs
    Frosting:
    1 cup sugar
    5 tablespoons butter
    $1/_3$ cup milk
    6 ounces semi-sweet chocolate

Cake: Preheat oven to 350 degrees. Grease and flour a 9" x 13" pan. In large bowl, combine all cake ingredients together and stir until well mixed. Pour into prepared pan and bake 45 to 55 minutes, until center springs back when lightly touched. Remove from oven and cool completely. *Frosting:* In small saucepan combine sugar, butter and milk; bring to a boil, stirring constantly for 1 minute. Remove from heat and stir in chocolate until smooth. Pour over cake in pan.

"A very easy and delicious cake! The frosting is wonderful!"

Gage Hewes   **South Pasadena High School, South Pasadena, CA**

Contributors

Names • Schools

Index

Categories • Recipes

30 **Minutes** or **Less**  CALIFORNIA
Cookbook

1907 Skycrest Drive
Fullerton, CA 92831

Please send me _____ copy(ies) of *30 Minutes or Less* at **$9.95** ea. (includes tax and postage).
Make checks payable to *California Cookbook Company.*

Enclosed is my check for _____ book(s) at **$9.95** ea $_____.

Name _____

Address _____

City _____ State _____ Zip _____

30 **Minutes** or **Less**  CALIFORNIA
Cookbook

1907 Skycrest Drive
Fullerton, CA 92831

Please send me _____ copy(ies) of *30 Minutes or Less* at **$9.95** ea. (includes tax and postage).
Make checks payable to *California Cookbook Company.*

Enclosed is my check for _____ book(s) at **$9.95** ea $_____.

Name _____

Address _____

City _____ State _____ Zip _____

30 **Minutes** or **Less**  CALIFORNIA
Cookbook

1907 Skycrest Drive
Fullerton, CA 92831

Please send me _____ copy(ies) of *30 Minutes or Less* at **$9.95** ea. (includes tax and postage).
Make checks payable to *California Cookbook Company.*

Enclosed is my check for _____ book(s) at **$9.95** ea $_____.

Name _____

Address _____

City _____ State _____ Zip _____